5 40

THE WORLD'S CLASSICS

GREEK LYRIC POETRY

M. L. WEST was formerly Professor of Greek at Royal
Holloway and Bedford New College, London, and is
now a Senior Research Fellow at All Souls College,
Oxford.

THE WORLD'S CLASSICS

Greek Lyric Poetry

The poems and fragments of the Greek iambic,
elegiac, and melic poets (excluding Pindar and
Bacchylides) down to 450 BC

Translated with Introduction and Notes by
M. L. WEST

Oxford   New York

OXFORD UNIVERSITY PRESS

1994

Oxford University Press, Walton Street, Oxford OX2 6DP

Oxford New York Toronto
Delhi Bombay Calcutta Madras Karachi
Kuala Lumpur Singapore Hong Kong Tokyo
Nairobi Dar es Salaam Cape Town
Melbourne Auckland Madrid

and associated companies in
Berlin Ibadan

Oxford is a trade mark of Oxford University Press

British Library Cataloguing in Publication Data
Data available

Library of Congress Cataloging in Publication Data
Greek lyric poetry: the poems and fragments of the Greek iambic,
elegiac, and melic poets (excluding Pindar and Bacchylides) down to
450 B.C. / *translated with introduction and notes by M. L. West.*
p. cm. — (The World's classics)
Includes bibliographical references (p.) and index.
1. Greek poetry—Translations into English. I. West, M. L.
(Martin Litchfield), 1937– . II. Series.
PA3622.W45 1994 884'.0108–dc20 94-5730
ISBN 0–19–282360–4

1 3 5 7 9 10 8 6 4 2

Printed in Great Britain by
BPC Paperbacks Ltd
Aylesbury, Bucks

CONTENTS

INTRODUCTION

'GREEK lyric poetry' is a conventional catch-all term covering more or less all the Greek poetry of the centuries down to 350 BC apart from epic, didactic, and other verse composed in hexameters, and drama. It cannot be considered a single genre. It is commonly subdivided into melic poetry, elegy, and iambus. But this division is not without its problems.

'Melic' means 'for song'; but song covers such a wide range, from little personal ditties to solemn choral cantatas, that this is still far from being a unified category. In any case, it is not really logical to distinguish 'melic' poetry from elegy and iambus, since most elegy was sung, and some iambus.

Elegy, at least, is easy to define. It is defined by its metre, the elegiac couplet, and whatever is composed in this metre for recitation or song is classed as elegy. It should be pointed out that the term does not carry the mournful associations that it has in the context of English literature.

As for iambus, it sounds as if it might be another metrical category, and indeed much of the verse that belongs under this heading is in iambic metre—much, but not all. The metre that we call iambic was so named because it was typical of 'iambus', not the other way round. 'Iambus' originally designated the entertaining monologues and songs performed at certain popular festivals of Demeter and Dionysus, which were typically ludicrous, scurrilous, or bawdy.

The general term 'lyric' ought to mean 'accompanied by the lyre'. But this again is inexact. It is true that most of this poetry was sung or recited to an instrumental accompaniment, but the instrument was not always a lyre. In many cases it was the *aulos*, a sort of oboe, two of which were played at once by a single player (the aulete), as was the custom with this instrument all over the ancient Near East. This is the instrument that countless writers on the Greeks have erroneously called a flute. The flute was not altogether unknown in antiquity, but the reader may take it that every reference he has ever seen to flutes or flute-girls in an ancient Greek context ought to have been to oboes and oboists. Besides the lyre and the *aulos*, which were always the principal Greek instruments, we should also mention the harp, which is referred to by a few poets (Sappho, Alcaeus, Anacreon) and was presumably sometimes used by them as an alternative to the lyre.

A solo singer accompanied himself on the lyre or harp, or was accompanied by an aulete. Elegy in particular was commonly sung to the *auloi*, in convivial gatherings where every guest was expected to sing something and a male or female aulete (a slave, or hired) was on hand to provide the musical accompaniment for those who were unable to play a stringed instrument for themselves. Choral song, which had its place mainly at festivals or other special occasions, was accompanied in some cases by the lyre, in others by the *auloi*, in others, apparently, by lyre and *auloi* simultaneously. In all kinds of song, the instrumental accompaniment served principally to support the vocal melody, with little embellishment.

To the modern reader the term 'lyric' may suggest a particular kind of literary style or mood. The body of Greek verse that we put together under this label, however, is very diverse in character. It includes every kind of song, with the exceptions of epic and drama already noted; and song is, after all, a medium almost as wide and varied in scope as speech. Epic and tragic poetry are focused on the mythical past. Some of this 'lyric' poetry too consists of mythic narrative, and allusions to the old myths are liable to appear anywhere. But what we have here above all is the poetry of the present, the poetry in which people express their feelings and ideas about all their current concerns: their personal loves or enmities, their hopes, fears, and complaints, matters affecting their circle of friends or their whole town. It is all social poetry, in the sense that although some poets looked forward to their work being preserved for the future, it was all intended initially for oral delivery (whether sung or recited) before an audience, private or public, in a specific setting. It was always a medium of communication to others, not a matter of poets committing their secret thoughts to paper to be published at some later time if at all. Even where a poem is nominally addressed to a single individual, or takes the form of a prayer addressed to a god, we can assume that it was in fact intended to be heard by a group.

Much of this poetry is of high quality; some of the poets counted among the finest that Greece produced. It is our misfor-

tune that most of their work has perished. We have some com-
plete poems, but for the most part there are only fragments, of
varying extent and completeness, preserved either on remnants
of ancient papyrus rolls or as quotations embedded in the texts
of later prose writers. All that was transmitted through the
Middle Ages in its own manuscript tradition was a collection of
the Victory Odes of Pindar and a collection of elegiac verse
labelled as 'Theognis', consisting in fact of anthologized
excerpts from various poets of whom Theognis was only one.
However, the situation is better than it used to be. New papyrus
fragments continue to be published, and this is one area of
Greek literature in which our knowledge has increased signific-
antly over the years. But we still have only a small fraction of
what circulated in antiquity.

In this volume I have translated all the surviving remains of
iambic, elegiac, and melic poetry down to about 450 BC, except
for the works of Pindar and Bacchylides, who require volumes
to themselves; I omit only such fragments as are too small or
broken to convey any intelligible image or idea. Many of the
lesser fragments that I do translate may perhaps be thought too
uninformative to justify their inclusion. But collectively, I think,
they do help to fill out our picture of the range of each poet's
subject-matter and poetic manner.

I have taken 450 BC as the notional limiting date because the
poetry of the succeeding period is somewhat different in charac-
ter, more self-conscious, less spontaneous in feeling and expres-
sion; there are no very major figures among its poets. The earlier
poetry, on the other hand, apart from the intrinsic beauty that
characterizes much of it—only imperfectly conveyed by a trans-
lation, but I hope not altogether obscured—is of particular inter-
est because so much of it shows us real Greeks speaking their
minds in a wide range of circumstances. We have virtually no
contemporary prose literature, and we rely on lyric above all
for evidence of the beliefs, attitudes, and opinions most preval-
ent in those times.

It is also an important source of information about historical
events. Ancient authors themselves, writers such as Aristotle
and Plutarch, depended largely on Tyrtaeus for their under-
standing of happenings in seventh-century Sparta, and on
Solon for their understanding of Athenian affairs half a century

later; we have the passages that these writers saw fit to quote
from the poets as evidence. Various other wars, political crises,
and revolutions are intermittently lit up by the lyric fragments,
and even where these add nothing to our knowledge of what
happened, they may give us a valuable insight into the emotions
aroused by the events, the hopes and forebodings, the exulta-
tion or the chagrin. The most recent additions to the corpus, a
series of papyrus fragments from elegies of Simonides, include
our first extended contemporary account of the days leading up
to the Battle of Plataea: a clearly poeticized account, but precious
to the historian.

I have arranged the material on a broadly chronological basis,
under the rubrics 'seventh century', 'seventh to sixth century',
and so on. We have one two-line fragment that is attributed to
a poet as early as the second half of the eighth century, **Eumelus**
of Corinth, but there is room for doubt as to whether it is really
so old. Otherwise, the earliest poets represented belong to the
middle of the seventh century. They are the elegists Callinus
of Ephesus and Tyrtaeus of Sparta, and the iambic poets
('iambographers') Archilochus of Paros and Semonides of
Amorgos.

Archilochus ranked in antiquity as one of the greatest of
poets, worthy to be named beside Homer and Hesiod. His
native island of Paros in the middle of the Aegean was one of
the chief centres of the worship of Demeter, goddess of agricul-
ture, and in association with this cult there was a local tradition
of iambus: scurrilous and erotic recitations and songs performed
at particular festivals, originally, no doubt, with the idea of pro-
moting fertility by means of explicit sexuality. Certainly, explicit
sexual (and in some authors scatological) material was admitted
by the iambographers to a degree that no other branch of literat-
ure tolerated apart from comedy, which was itself in origin asso-
ciated with fertility rituals. In iambus, sex and scatology typic-
ally appear in the framework of first-person narratives. The
speaker or singer (possibly costumed in the role of a stock
figure) regaled the audience with accounts of extravagant orgies
or other escapades in which he claimed to have taken part. He
named women whom he had seduced or who had eagerly given
themselves to him. If these were real women, the allegations
must have been exceedingly embarrassing and shaming to them

and their families, and there are stories of iambographers' victims being driven to suicide by the publicity; but there is something to be said for the view that the persons named were in some cases fictitious. Archilochus' iambi were particularly concerned with one Lycambes and his two daughters, one of whom was called Neobule. The reader will notice several mentions of them, and will easily identify other fragments as belonging to the iambic genre.

But by no means all of Archilochus' poetry can be ascribed to this genre. Much of it represents his reactions to current events, military, political, and personal. There is affectionate banter with friends, bristly remonstrance with enemies, satirical comment on public figures, solemn lament for men lost at sea, vivid references to impending or recent battles. The variety of tone is wide, but Archilochus always comes across as a man of spirit. A number of fragments refer to Thasos, the north Aegean island that was colonized by the Parians: Archilochus spent part of his life there, and was involved in fighting with Thracian tribes on the nearby mainland.

Semonides of Amorgos (not to be confused with the more famous Simonides of Ceos) is a much more indistinct figure. A few of the lesser fragments indicate that his iambus too included elements of obscene narrative. The two main fragments, however, might be put under the heading of popular philosophy. One of them, the so-called 'satire on women', is the longest piece of non-hexameter verse that we have in Greek from before the fifth century. Its 118 lines are almost a complete poem, with only a few lines lost at the end. The generally unfavourable picture of women reflects an attitude that was common. But we should remember that the piece was designed as a conventional entertainment. The theme of woman as a plague appeared in other iambographers too, and it should be compared to routine jokes about mothers-in-law in the more vulgar kind of modern comedy rather than being seen as an expression of personal bitterness.

Callinus of Ephesus and **Tyrtaeus** of Sparta, although they lived on opposite sides of the Aegean, wrote elegies of very similar character. Both use the medium to exhort their fellow citizens to fight to the death in defence of their community, winning glory and averting shame. These poems, perhaps more than Homer, give us an idea of what it felt like to be a young man in early Greece, faced with the prospect of going into battle—both the physical dangers and the moral pressures.

Callinus' audience seem to be unprepared for war, perhaps enjoying their symposium. Tyrtaeus, on the other hand, speaks as if his hearers are ready drawn up on the battlefield, and it is not impossible that this was the actual situation. We know that three centuries later, when Tyrtaeus was an established classic, Spartan armies were made to listen to recitations of his works. The conflict for which at least some of his poems were composed was the Second Messenian War. Messene, the fertile country beyond the mountains to the west of Sparta, had been brought under Spartan domination two generations previously, in the late eighth century, and it had now risen in revolt. The Spartans succeeded in subduing it again, but not without some difficulty. At the same period they were suffering from internal political troubles. The poor found themselves without sufficient land, and clamoured for a redistribution. The authority of the city's two kings and of the council of elders was threatened. Here again we see Tyrtaeus playing a role as propagandist. In a poem to which later writers gave the title *Eunomia* ('Law and Order') he reminded the people of the divine authority on which the constitution rested, and he called for obedience to the rulers and an end to discord.

Later in the seventh century we find **Mimnermus** of Smyrna again using elegy to rouse his people to the fight, perhaps against the Lydians, who had attacked Smyrna before and, about 600 BC, succeeded in destroying it. But Mimnermus was better remembered for poetry celebrating the delights of love and youth. According to later reports, loved ones of both sexes were named in his poems, and indeed both he and Solon speak of the love of boys and women as if they were complementary. But the more personal parts of his love poetry have not survived, only anthology excerpts containing general reflections on the subject.

Towards the end of the century we encounter our first substantial specimens of choral poetry. They come from the Partheneia (girls' songs) of **Alcman**, composed for Spartan girls' choruses to sing and dance to at certain festivals, and they give glimpses of a very different side of Spartan life from those that concerned Tyrtaeus. The longest piece (fragment 1) comes from a papyrus in the Louvre which was one of the first Greek literary papyri to be discovered; it was published in 1855. The text indicates that the chorus consists of ten girls and that a religious ceremony of some sort is in progress. It is sometimes thought that the chorus was in competition against another. There are mythological and moralizing passages, and a fair amount about the girls themselves and their finery, with especial praise of the beauty of two who are attending to the sacrifice. One of them is even portrayed as the girls' heart-throb. This was apparently a conventional element in these Spartan Partheneia, as it appears also in a fragment from another one, with a different girl named.

It is in the work of **Sappho**, of course, that the theme of love between women is most famously in evidence. Most of her songs were composed for private pleasure in her house, where, it seems, a circle of unmarried women or girls regularly made music and sang. The nature of the arrangement is not clear, but the most plausible view is that these young women were entrusted to Sappho by their parents for instruction in music and perhaps also in letters. On occasion they sang in public at weddings or festivals. A certain number of the fragments are from wedding songs or religious performances. But the majority are from more intimate compositions, and concerned with personal matters. There is little mention of men, apart from bridegrooms in the wedding songs. It is very much a women's world that is reflected. When Sappho speaks of the old myths about Troy, they are seen through a woman's eyes. It is Hector's wedding that stirs her imagination, not his prowess on the battlefield; Helen is viewed with some sympathy, as a woman whose priorities were upset by love.

Alcaeus was contemporary with Sappho, and lived in the same town of Mytilene on the island of Lesbos. Yet there is no certain indication of any contact between them. If Sappho's is a woman's world, Alcaeus' is no less decidedly a man's. His songs are mostly composed for drinking-parties with male cronies. There are hymns to gods, celebrations of the pleasures of wine and love (of boys), and, above all, songs about fighting and politics. Like many other Greek towns in the seventh and sixth centuries, Mytilene was going through a period of instability. One leader after another seized power, or was raised to power on a wave of popular support. We hear of successive administrations by Melanchrus, Myrsilus, and Pittacus. Alcaeus belonged to an established landowning family and, in shifting alliances with others of his class, and at one point with a neighbouring foreign power (Lydia), he struggled in opposition to the popular leaders. But the city was out of sympathy with him, and he found himself evicted from his estates and banished to another part of the island.

Theognis of Megara is in some ways a similar figure: a 'squirearch', a man of standing in his city, whose public actions, however, arouse some discontent; a man who sings to his drinking-comrades of his anxieties about the political situation; a man of cliques, who finds himself betrayed by those he trusted, dispossessed of his land in a democratic revolution, an impoverished and embittered exile dreaming of revenge. His allusions to current situations seem best to fit the last decades of the seventh century, though later chroniclers date him in the middle of the sixth. Not all of his elegies were political. Some of them (or, to be more exact, some of the surviving excerpts) contain general moral advice; some are amatory. In all these categories Theognis habitually addresses his poems to his friend Cyrnus, also called Polypaïdes. The appearance of one or other of these two names is the chief criterion that enables us to identify Theognis' verse among the much larger collection of elegiac excerpts transmitted as his. It is not that an excerpt lacking an address to Cyrnus cannot be by Theognis, but that, as we can see that the collection contains excerpts from Tyrtaeus, Mimnermus, Solon, and others, some as late as the fifth century, it is only prudent to treat as anonymous any piece for which we have no positive indication of authorship. I have accordingly separated 'Theognis' from 'Anonymous Theognidea'. In the latter section I have taken out those pieces which can be ascribed to a named poet, and also the duplications that are a feature of the collection: the same item often appears twice (with some textual divergences), as a result of the conflation of different ancient anthologies.

The anonymous Theognidea have a fascination of their own, even if they cannot be grouped round a single personality. Many of them were clearly composed for the symposium, and many more are on the subject of drinking or making merry. It was the custom in some circles for the guests to be wittily rude to each other, and we see at least one example of this (lines 453–6). Other pieces are reflective or philosophic, even dialectical. Many—especially those gathered at the end of the collection (lines 1231–389)—are love poems, mostly addressed to unnamed boys. The value of the collection as a whole is that it may be taken as a representative cross-section of the elegiac poetry written for sympotic and other social settings in the sixth and early fifth centuries. It is here, out of all the material gathered in this volume, that we come closest to the ordinary man and his views on life, friendship, society, fate, death.

At the end of the seventh century and the beginning of the sixth we encounter the first known Athenian poet: none other than the famous statesman **Solon**. Much of his verse, like that of Tyrtaeus and Theognis, is concerned with the public affairs of his city. He played an important part in those affairs. Inequalities between rich and poor had produced a critical situation. The misery and resentment of the under-class threatened to erupt in revolution and to throw up some popular dictator, as had happened at Megara and other places. Solon, after passing a series of comments and warnings on these dangers, in poems that evidently circulated well beyond the confines of a private drinking-group, summoned a mass meeting, won its support, and was given powers to frame special laws to ease the situation. They brought some relief, but failed to please everyone, and in subsequent poems we hear Solon passionately defending his actions against more than one set of critics. The eloquence and vivid imagery of his poetry make it easy for us to understand how this man was able to dominate a crowd.

Alcman, Sappho, Alcaeus, Theognis, and Solon all belong under the heading 'seventh to sixth century' because they were (or may have been) active both before and after 600. But the rubric also covers a couple of poets whom we can only date vaguely to the later seventh *or* the sixth century. They are an obscure iambographer from Selinus in Sicily, one **Aristoxenus**, of whom a single line survives—quite a long one, it is true— and the author of the comic poem *Margites*, which was rather implausibly reputed to have been composed by Homer in a rare fit of drollery. It was in an irregular mixture of epic hexameter

and iambic lines, and it concerned a ridiculous ninny called
Margites and the ludicrous situations that he got himself into.
Ancient allusions indicate that the main episode dealt with Mar-
gites' wedding night. He had no idea what to do with his bride,
until she told him that a scorpion had bitten her between the
legs and that the wound could only be healed by the insertion
of a man's penis.

The numerous Greek colonies in the west, in Sicily and Italy,
naturally produced their own poets, and two major lyricists of
the sixth century came from that part of the world: Stesichorus
and Ibycus. **Stesichorus'** poems were narratives on legendary
subjects, composed on the most ample scale. We know that one
of them, the *Oresteia*, was divided into at least two books, and
a fragment of the *Song of Geryon* has a numeral in the margin
signifying 'line 1300'. These were in effect lyric epics, sung to
expansive strophic melodies. It used to be generally assumed
that this was choral poetry, but it now seems likely that Stesich-
orus performed it as a solo singer accompanying himself on the
lyre, possibly with a chorus of dancers. His themes included
several of Heracles' adventures, various episodes connected
with the Trojan War, its antecedents and aftermath, and legends
from central Greece. The fifth-century tragedians often drew
upon Stesichorus for material and for particular versions of
myths.

Ibycus came from Rhegium, the modern Reggio. He is clearly
no stranger to the Stesichorean tradition, but his poetry is much
more personal in orientation, often concerned with love. In the
amatory fragments we see some striking imagery, as well as
some rather distasteful baroque conceits. The longest extant
piece concludes with praise of Polycrates, son of Aeaces the
ruler of Samos, where Ibycus settled down as a court poet.
Polycrates himself came to power in about 538, and under him
the prestige of Samos reached a height it never attained before
or since.

Anacreon too enjoyed the patronage of this Samian dynasty;
Aeaces is said to have made him Polycrates' music-teacher. Ana-
creon, an Ionian from Abdera, must be counted one of the very
finest of the lyric poets. No wild outpouring of passion here,
but feeling tempered by humour and expressed in little songs
of exquisite craftsmanship. Posterity saw Anacreon as the arche-

typal merry old soul, the cheerful devotee of wine and love, tottering home from the party with garland askew and with a pretty boy to guide him. Many centuries after his death, a new genre of 'Anacreontic' poetry sprang into life. From about the first century of our era down to Byzantine times, poets composed simple sympotic songs in the spirit of Anacreon (as they understood it), in metres derived from his, and in some cases referring to him by name or even adopting his persona. These later Anacreontea exercised a powerful influence on European literature from the sixteenth century onward; until 1834 they were always included in editions of Anacreon's fragments, and it was only by degrees that their spuriousness came to be agreed by all.

Polycrates fell in about 522, and Anacreon spent his latter years at Athens. His patron there was Hipparchus, the younger brother of the dictator Hippias. Other, more avant-garde poets in Hipparchus' circle were Lasus of Hermione, who was interested in musical theory and may actually have invented the word 'music' (mousikē), and Simonides of Ceos, of whom more anon.

A few minor names from the sixth century must be mentioned here. Asius of Samos was mainly significant as an epic poet, but one enigmatic elegiac fragment survives. Demodocus, a caustic wit, came from the small Aegean island of Leros. His habit of introducing his mots with the phrase 'Another from Demodocus' was a satirical borrowing from an earnest moralizing poem in hexameters current in neighbouring Miletus, where successive admonitions began with 'Another from Phocylides'. Practically nothing is known of Pythermus of Teos, or of the iambographer Ananius, who referred to a popular song by Pythermus.

The last of the three major iambographers (the other two being Archilochus and Semonides) is Hippōnax of Ephesus, active towards the end of the sixth century. The traditional iambic element of first-person sexual narrative is well represented in his fragments. But the tone is noticeably different from that in the seventh-century writers of iambus. Hipponax is more obviously setting out to be funny. He presents himself as a vulgar fellow, given to brawling and burglary. His reported adventures are not just erotic but picaresque, sordid, and farcical. The whole way of life that he describes is low-class and shabby. The effect is enhanced by his use of vulgar language, with an admixture of foreign words that were presumably current in the colloquial speech of Ephesus. Just as Archilochus has a favourite enemy, Lycambes, so has Hipponax: it is Bupalus, a sculptor, reputed to have antagonized the poet by caricaturing him. Hipponax claims to have enjoyed wild nights with Bupalus' mistress Ārētē.

The long life of **Xenophanes** of Colophon easily bridges the sixth and fifth centuries. He is the first poet of Greece (and of the world, I fancy) whose year of birth can be stated more or less exactly. This is because he tells us that he was 25 ('if I can claim to know the truth of it') when he left his Ionian home for a life of wandering through Greece, and it is probable that what uprooted him was the Persian capture of Colophon in about 540. His wanderings have lasted a further 67 years, so he is still writing verse at the age of 92, in about 473 BC. Xenophanes plays a role in histories of philosophy because of his highly radical speculations on cosmology and theology. These he expounded in hexameter verse, which falls outside the scope of the present volume. But the elegiac fragments themselves give a hint of his opinionated and argumentative nature, and of his self-esteem.

Simonides of Ceos, a few years younger than Xenophanes, also attained a ripe old age: he boasts that, octogenarian though he is, he has a matchless memory. In him we encounter a professional lyricist of a new type, a poet who acquires a national reputation and openly trades on it to get custom from everywhere. Hipparchus of Athens has been mentioned as one of Simonides' patrons. He had many others, in Euboea, Thessaly, Aegina, Sparta, Sicily, and Italy—men of wealth and standing, who could afford the high fees he was notorious for charging. It was a pattern to be followed by his nephew Bacchylides and by Pindar. Like them, Simonides composed choral odes celebrating his patrons' victories at the great national sports meetings such as the Olympics. But he composed many other kinds of melic poetry too, as well as elegy. In more than one genre he celebrated the great critical battles of the Persian Wars. These wars gave Greece a new consciousness of national identity, and Simonides was the first poet to give it expression.

After Simonides I have placed another group of minor figures.

Susarion of Megara was cited by Megarian antiquarians to sub-stantiate the claim that comedy was invented at Megara, not at Athens. But the fragment quoted must be assigned to the genus iambus rather than comedy, and the man's date is quite uncer-tain. **Apollodorus** was an Athenian choral poet, active around 500 BC. **Cydias** may have been another, though the evidence is frail. **Pratinas** of Phlius is somewhat better known, mainly as an early contributor to Athenian tragedy and satyric drama.

After these the reader will come upon an interesting collection of stanzas under the heading **Anonymous Party Songs**. Num-bers 884–908 circulated as a collection in antiquity. They were evidently popular items sung by guests at Athenian symposia in the fifth century. Many of them have the same metrical struc-ture, and were no doubt sung to a particular well-known tune. A number of them celebrate a famous event of the year 514, when Hipparchus—that patron of outstanding poets, but brother of an increasingly unpopular dictator—was assassinated at a public festival by Harmodius and Aristogeiton. Three years later the dictator himself was ousted and democracy was estab-lished. As the songs show, these events came to be somewhat run together in the popular memory, as if Hipparchus had been the tyrant and his death had at once brought the regime to an end. The song-book also contained two or three items from identifiable poets (Alcaeus, Praxilla), which I have left out because they appear elsewhere in their due place.

The **Praxilla** just mentioned was a poetess from Sicyon in the north-east Peloponnese. She was credited on the one hand with songs suitable for the symposium—which might suggest a cour-tesan—and on the other hand with choral poetry and hymns, which would point rather to a respectable, matronly chorus-leader. It is possible that two different women of the same name have been confused, or else that Praxilla's authorship of the sympotic songs, about which the ancients seem to have enter-tained some doubts, was a fiction. Another early fifth-century woman poet from the same region, the Argive **Telesilla**, is more unequivocally portrayed as a lady of standing in her city and a leader of female choruses. Before the Hellenistic age, this was the role in which the woman poet could most naturally emerge into the daylight as a public figure. Sappho too, we recall, had such a role in her society.

Timocreon of Rhodes wrote songs of a rather personal nature. It is not clear for what sort of occasion he wrote them, but he evidently hoped for and to some extent obtained a nation-wide hearing. A couple of his fragments are of historical interest for their references to events of the years *c*.479–467, and in particular for invective against Themistocles.

The last elegist included in this volume is **Euenus** of Paros. It must be confessed that the identification of this man and of the fragments to be ascribed to him requires a certain measure of faith. Plato and Aristotle refer to a Parian sophist and rhetorician Euenus, a contemporary of Socrates, and Aristotle quotes verses of his. One of these is virtually identical with a line that appears in the Theognidea in one of three poems addressed to a certain Simonides. It is a reasonable guess that those three poems are by the same poet, and a slightly more risky inference that he was Aristotle's Euenus. But if the Simonides addressed is the famous poet, the author must have been of mature age by about 470, too early for the sophist; and that is the sort of date suggested by the style of the poems and by their presence in the Theognidean collection. It may be that Aristotle confused an older and a younger Euenus. A further complication is that there was at least one, perhaps more than one, later epigrammatist called Euenus. Certain verses cited under this name have to be assigned, as between the various claimants, on rather subjective criteria.

Lamprocles, an Athenian musician, probably flourished a little before the middle of the fifth century. His hymn to Athena is cited by Aristophanes as a 'classic' piece in the good old traditional style. Lamprocles perhaps sang it to his own lyre accompaniment at the great city festival of Athena, the Panathenaea, in the competition for citharodes. The citharode, a professional who sang to the *cithara* (a grander kind of lyre than the ones used in domestic music-making), was the most highly acclaimed sort of musical performer, admired both for his mastery of the instrument and for his fine singing. The citharodes looked back to **Terpander** of Lesbos (*c*.680–650) as the first great exponent of the art, and attributed many achievements to him: increasing the number of the lyre's strings from four to seven, inventing new scales and rhythms, establishing rules of musical form, and so on. Much of this was no doubt constructed by projecting classical citharodes' practices back on to the first famous citharode. Similarly, when Terpander is named as the source of a couple of hymn fragments, we should probably take them to come from a body of 'traditional' pieces that citharodes of the classical period availed themselves of and ascribed collectively to Terpander. There is no good evidence that actual songs of his were handed down.

A few pages of **anonymous** fragments conclude the volume. Most of them are anonymous because the ancient authors who quote them omit to specify where they are quoting from. But the groups headed 'work songs', 'play songs', and 'ritual songs' fall into a different category. These are the pieces generally labelled 'carmina popularia' in scholarly editions. They were 'popular' in the sense that they were not thought of as belonging to any particular author or performer, but were sung traditionally to accompany certain activities: routine labour, children's games, local religious rituals. They did not circulate in book form, and our knowledge of them is confined to the few that ancient writers chance to quote. These are usually writers of the Hellenistic or Roman period, and we cannot say how old the songs are. Some of them certainly go back to the classical age, and in general they are characterized by a simplicity of language and metre that would not be out of place in the sixth or fifth century. If these actual pieces did not exist so early, they may be taken as samples of a basically timeless category of folk-song that certainly must have existed from the beginning. Even the child Homer, we can assume, played singing games.

The translation

I have tried to produce readable verse translations while rendering as faithfully as possible the thought and the spirit of the originals. This means, for example, reproducing the metaphors and images used in the Greek, so far as they can be made intelligible to the modern reader, and not importing new ones. Minor shifts are occasionally necessary, as when Alcaeus (frag. 351) uses a metaphor from an ancient board game that has no modern equivalent, and speaks of someone 'moving the stone (counter) from the holy line'. The point is that this was a move made only in the last resort, so the appropriate translation will be 'playing his final card'. No one will be misled, I hope, into supposing that the Greeks played cards.

Another necessity sometimes forced upon the translator is the use of words or expressions that have an old-fashioned air, simply because they correspond better than any current idiom to the Greek concept. This arises particularly in moral and ethical contexts. There is a very common set of words in Greek, *dikē, dikaios, adikos*, which the student is taught to translate as 'justice, just, unjust'. But these renderings are quite inadequate, as 'justice' in English is a quality of the law, judges, or others in a position to allocate some resource among claimants, whereas *dikē* is a property of anyone who abides by the law, deals fairly with his neighbours, and so on. The word that best catches it is the biblical-sounding 'righteousness'. Again, the early Greek poets very often contrast the 'good' man (*agathos* or *esthlos*) with the 'bad' man (*kakos* or *deilos*). In English, 'good' and 'bad' applied to persons refer simply to moral character, unless some further qualification is added (as in 'a good man in a crisis'). But in early Greek the terms refer predominantly to social status, inherited wealth, breeding, or the lack of these, often with the assumption that moral worth is their natural concomitant. In many cases *agathos* is best represented by a phrase such as 'man of quality', 'man of class', or 'man of worth', and *kakos* by 'rogue', 'rapscallion', 'bum', 'man of low degree', or the like. It should go without saying that it is not practicable, in a work such as this, always to translate the same word or phrase in the same way; nor have I made any particular effort to do so.

I have tried to give some idea of the metrical variety of the originals. Sometimes I have actually imitated the ancient metres, in so far as it is possible to imitate quantitative measures (based on the contrast of longer and shorter syllables) in a language where the prosodic opposition is between stressed and unstressed elements. For example, the metre of Sappho, fragment 44,

$$- \times - \cup \cup - \cup \cup - \cup \cup - \cup -$$

is meant to be reflected in my line

Só the hérald Idaéus arríved with the méssage swíft,

and that of Alcaeus, fragment 342,

$$- \cup - \cup \cup - - \cup \cup - - \cup \cup - \cup -$$

by my

Lét the víne be the fírst fruít-tree you plánt: óthers can waít
   their túrn.

In other cases, without attempting to reproduce the original
metrical pattern, I have tried to convey some idea of the general
effect, for example, by using a strophe of two shorter lines and
one longer one where that is the structure of the original. In
translating the many poems composed in elegiac couplets, I
have usually used iambic lines with alternately six and five
stresses, though in a few cases I have used five-stress verses
for both lines of the couplet, relying on indentation to indicate
the alternation.

   It has been an enjoyable task. I do not delude myself that all
parts of the end product are likely to give equal pleasure to the
reader. But if I have succeeded in opening any eyes, ears, or
hearts to some portion of the manifold beauty, wisdom, and wit
that shines from these precious remnants of a brilliant culture of
long ago, I shall be well content.

NOTE ON THE NUMERATION OF FRAGMENTS

I HAVE given the fragments the numbers that they bear in the scholarly editions currently regarded as standard, namely: for the iambic and elegiac poets, M. L. West, *Iambi et Elegi Graeci* (2nd edn., Oxford, 1989–92); for the Lesbian poets, E.-M. Voigt, *Sappho et Alcaeus* (Amsterdam, 1971) (the numbers are nearly all the same as in the older edition of E. Lobel and D. L. Page, *Poetarum Lesbiorum Fragmenta* (Oxford, 1955)); for other melic poets, D. L. Page, *Poetae Melici Graeci* (Oxford, 1962) and *Supplementum Lyricis Graecis* (Oxford, 1974; numbers prefixed by S). Page's numerations are taken over in M. Davies, *Poetarum Melicorum Graecorum Fragmenta* (Oxford, 1991), of which one volume has so far appeared, containing Alcman, Stesichorus, and Ibycus. The Theognidea are provided with the continuous line-numbering used in all modern editions.

A row of three dots (. . .) indicates a gap in the preserved text; a row of five dots indicates a single missing line. Words partly or wholly restored by conjecture are enclosed in square brackets.

BIBLIOGRAPHICAL NOTE

C. M. B O W R A' s *Greek Lyric Poetry* (2nd edn., Oxford, 1961) long did duty as the standard survey of this field for English readers. We now have the relevant chapters by various hands in *The Cambridge History of Classical Literature*, i: *Greek Literature* (Cambridge, 1985), 117–244, with the extensive bibliographies on pp. 728–46, and a good brief account by E. L. Bowie in *The Oxford History of the Classical World* (Oxford, 1986), 99–112. H. Fränkel, *Early Greek Poetry and Philosophy* (New York, 1975), also deserves a warm recommendation. D. A. Campbell, *The Golden Lyre* (London, 1983), discusses the poets' treatment of a series of themes—love, death, politics, etc.

Two excellent books that set the poets in a wider historical and social context are A. R. Burn, *The Lyric Age of Greece* (London, 1960), and O. Murray, *Early Greece* (London, 1980).

For all aspects of musical performance—singing, instruments, rhythms, scales, melody—I may refer to my *Ancient Greek Music* (Oxford, 1992).

Seventh Century

ARCHILOCHUS

Epodes*

1. *To Lycambes*

172   Papa Lycambes, what d'you mean by this?
            Who has unhinged your wits
        that used to be so sound? Now you turn out
            the big laugh of the town.

173   You've turned your back on the great bond
            of shared salt and table . . .

174   There is a tale men tell
        of how a vixen with an eagle once
            made friends . . .

(*But one day the eagle flew down and carried off one of the vixen's cubs,*)

175   taking it to his sons,
        and the two fledgelings fell upon a feast
            unlovely, on the high
        crag where they had their nest.

176   'You see where that high crag is, rugged, harsh?
            That's where he sits, and holds
        your challenge in contempt.'

177 (*The vixen prays:*)

            'O father Zeus, thine is the power in heaven,
                and thou dost oversee
            men's deeds, wicked and lawful; all creatures'
                    rights
                and wrongs are thy concern.'

(The prayer did not go unanswered. Some time later the eagle seized a piece of meat from a sacrificial altar,)

179   brought it and set it down before his sons,
          a feast doom-laden . . .

180   There was a spark of fire in it . . .

(And the nest went up in flames, fledglings and all.)

181   . . . aware of the disaster
          . . . helpless . . .
          . . . took his way swiftly through the air
          wheeling on speedy wings.
          . . . Now, do you expect . . . ?

2. *To a Member of the College of Heralds*

185   I want to tell you folk a tale, your Honour,
          —oh, it's a mournful dispatch!
      A monkey left the other animals
          and wandered alone in the wild,
      and there a crafty fox came up to him,
          bearing a heart full of guile.

(The fox said it had found a treasure which the monkey ought to have, in view of his distinguished status, and led him to a trap that a man had baited with meat.)

225   'Pray go ahead: you are of noble birth!'

             .   .   .

186   pressing the bar of the trap.

(The monkey was caught in an undignified posture, releasing the meat for the fox. He remonstrated with the fox, who answered:)

187   'But oh sir Monkey—with a bum like that,
          thinking so much of yourself?'

             .   .   .

3. *To an Ex-mistress*

188   Your tender skin has lost its former bloom,
          dries out in furrows; ugly age
      makes you its prey. Sweet charm from your fair
          face
      has hopped it. After all, the winds
      of many winters have assaulted you,
          and many a time . . .

189   and many a sightless eel have you taken in

190   and I used to explore your rugged glens
               in my full-blooded youth . . .

191   Such was the lust for sex that, worming in
               under my heart, quite blinded me
           and robbed me of my young wits . . . .

4. *Encounter in a Meadow*

196   . . . No, my dear friend,
           I'm overcome by crippling desire.

196*a*   '. . . holding entirely off . . .

           If you can't wait and your desire is urgent,
           there's somebody else at our house
           now longing for a man,

           a lovely slender girl, there's nothing wrong
           (if I'm any judge) with her looks.
           Why not make friends with her?'

           That's what she said, and here's how I replied:
           'Daughter of Amphimedo,
           that lady fine and true

           whom now the mouldy earth has taken in,
           the love-goddess offers young men
           a range of joys besides

           the sacrament, and one of them will serve.
           We'll talk of all this, you and I,
           at leisure, when . . .

           . . . grows dark, and may God be our aid.
           I'll do it all just as you say.

           But please, my dear, don't grudge it if I go
           under the arch, through the gates;
           I'll dock at the grass borders,

           be sure of that. Now as for Neoboule,
           someone else have her. Dear me,
           she's past ripe, twice your age;

her girlhood's flower has shed its petals, lost
all the enchantment it had.
She never got enough;

she's proved her . . .'s measure, crazy woman.
Keep her away—for the crows!
I pray no friend of mine

would have me marry somebody like her
and give all the neighbours a laugh.
No, you're the one I want.

You're not untrustworthy, you're not two-faced,
but she's so precipitate, she
makes friends with crowds of men.

I don't want babies blind and premature,
like the proverbial bitch,
from showing too much haste.'

That's what I said; and then I took the girl,
and laying her down in the flowers,
with my soft-textured cloak

I covered her; my arm cradled her neck,
while she in her fear like a fawn
gave up the attempt to run.

Gently I touched her breasts, where the young
      flesh
peeped from the edge of her dress,
her ripeness newly come,

and then, caressing all her lovely form,
I shot my hot energy off,
just brushing golden hairs.

Fragments of other epodes

168   Fitzdarling, delight of the people,
            I've got a funny story
          to tell you, my dearest companion,
            and I guarantee you'll like it.

184   She was a cheater—water in one hand,
            fire in the other.

197   Father Zeus, I had no wedding feast . . .

200   He won't get off scot-free from me.

201   The fox knows lots of tricks,
        the hedgehog only one—but it's a winner.

192 (*On a Shipwreck*)
        From fifty men Poseidon Hippios
        chose Koiranos to spare.

298   Among the gods Zeus is the trustiest seer,
        controlling the outcome himself.

Iambi

Erotic fragments

23   I replied:
        'Madam, you mustn't be at all afraid
        of ill repute. As for . . .
        I'll deal with it. Don't you be angry with me.
        You really think I'm such a wretch as that?
        You must have seen me as a low-class churl,
        not what I am and what my forebears were.
        I know the art of loving him that loves me,
        hating my hater and foulmouthing him
        with an ant's venom. So I'm quite sincere.
        This citadel that you are walking in
        was never sacked by any man, but now
        your spear has conquered it, yours is the glory:
        so be its queen, enjoy dominion.
        I dare say quite a few will envy you.'

48   Their nurse brought them along, with scented hair
        and bosoms, such that even an old man
        would have desired them. Oh Glaucus, . . .

30, 31 She had a myrtle-sprig and a beautiful rose
        that she was playing with; her hair hung down
        shading her shoulders and her upper back.

32   . . . right through the myrtle-spray.

36   They lay down in the shadow of the wall

37   There is this wall that runs all round the yard.

39   Every man rolled back his skin . . .

247   . . . his tender horn . . .

40   . . . wet mound of Venus . . .

41   Up and down she bounced
like a kingfisher flapping on a jutting rock.

42   Like a Thracian or Phrygian drinking beer through
      a tube
she sucked, stooped down, engaged too from
      behind.

43   And his dong
. . . flooded over like a Prienian
stall-fed donkey's . . .

44   . . . foam all round her mouth . . .

45   They stooped and spurted off
all their accumulated wantonness.

46   . . . through the tube into the vessel.

47   The virgin priestesses
with cudgels drove you away from the door.

60   O fortunate man, to have
such daughters to his name!

66   . . . a growth between the thighs . . .

67   I won't use surgery,
I know another sovereign remedy
for a growth of this description.

222   . . . and severed the tendons of his middle parts.

252   But the sinews of his wick
are ruptured . . .

118–20

I wish I had as sure a chance of fingering
     Neoboule—
the workman falling to his flask—and pressing
     tum to tummy
and thighs to thighs . . .
as sure as I know how to start the lovely round
     of singing
lord Dionysus' dithyramb when the wine has
     blitzed my brains in.

Political fragments

20 My tears are for Thasos' troubles, not Magnesia's.*

21 . . . while Thasos stands here like
 the spine of a donkey, wreathed with unkempt forest.

 It's not a beautiful or lovely place
22 or charming like the Siris river lands.*

 Erxias, how's that god-forsaken army
88 regrouping this time?
    Let the stone of Tantalus
91 not be poised above this island . . .

 into the fray. Zeus held the balance equal,
 not turning either of the fronts . . .
 earth ran with blood . . .

93 . . . the son of Pisistratus
 brought back these connoisseurs of lyre and pipe
 to Thasos, with a cargo of pure gold
 for bribing Thracian dogs. But then for sake
 of private gain they did a public harm.

94   By their battle line
 stood Athena favouringly, daughter of
   loud-thundering Zeus.
 She it was that stirred that much-lamented
   country's army's hearts.
 Fugitives that day were seeking billets in many
   different parts;
 they retreated many furlongs . . .
 . . . but the Olympian gods' intent . . .

96 Glaucus, which of the gods has turned your wits?
 Have a thought for this land . . .
 braving dangers with us . . .
 . . . your spear conquered . . .

98 . . . spears . . . broke their spirit . . .
 . . . Athena, daughter of Zeus.
 Round the high battlements their country's doom
 they fought off . . . there was set a looming
 bastion, impressive, that we built of stone

. . . men of Lesbos . . .
. . . put shields on their arms . . .
. . . Zeus the Olympians' . . .
With our slick spears we were inflicting woe,
but round the wall they busily set ladders,
their courage high. Loud boomed the ironclad
contrivance . . . alternate; streams of missiles . . .
Quivers no longer hid their store of death
. . . arrows, while they . . .
. . . twisting the sinews, drawing bows . . .

101   For seven of the enemy we overtook and slew,
a thousand of us claim the kill . . .

228   But as for Thasos, that thrice-wretched city . . .

102   All Greece's wretchedness is now drained down
to Thasos . . .

105   Glaucus, see,* the waves are rising and the deep
sea is disturbed;
all about the heights of Gyrae stands a towering
mass of cloud—
that's a sign of storm. I fall a prey to unexpected
fear.

106   . . . fast ships at sea
. . . let's untie the sheets and slacken sail.
Father Zeus, hold our wind fair and keep our
comrades safe, for then
when we land you'll have our thanks; and keep
the gusts and gales away,
don't hurl this new storm upon us as we fight the
churning waves
. . . but take thought on our behalf . . .

107   Many of them, I expect, the burning Dog-star will
parch up,
shining fiercely down . . .

108   Hear me, lord Hephaestus, to my supplication be
a favouring ally: grant the favours that are yours to
grant.

110 It's true what they say: the god of war's
impartial toward men.

111 And encourage the younger men; but victory's
under the gods' control.

114 I don't like an army commander who's tall, or goes
at a trot,
or one who has glamorous wavy hair, or trims his
beard a lot.
A shortish sort of chap, who's bandy-looking
round the shins,
he's my ideal, one full of guts, and steady on his
pins.

115 But now Leophilus is in charge, it's Leophilus' turn
to be king;
everything's clear for Leophilus,
pray silence for Leophilus,
and all that sort of thing.

Miscellaneous iambic fragments

19 'Gyges* and all his gold don't interest me.
I've never been prey to envy, I don't marvel
at heavenly things, or yearn for great dominion.
That's all beyond the sights of such as me.'

. . .

Thus quoth Charon the joiner . . .

24 Welcome back, . . . In a small ship you crossed
a mighty sea, and made it home from Gortyn.*
. . . I'm glad of this as well.
It wasn't the best of vessels that you came in,
. . . but God
held his hand over you, and now you're here
. . . I don't mind about the cargo,
if you are safe, whether it's gone for good
or whether there's some way to get it back.
I'd never find another friend like you,
if you'd been drowned at sea, or at the hands
of spearmen lost your manhood's glorious prime.
But now it stays in bloom, God's kept you safe

    . . . and see me left alone
    . . . prostrate in the gloom
    . . . I'm brought back to the light of day.

25   There is no single kind of human nature,
        but different things warm different people's hearts.
        For instance, Melesandros favours prick,
        Phalangios the cowherd is for . . .
        This revelation comes to you from me,
        no other prophet; Zeus the Olympians' father
        made me a . . . among men
        and a good one, whom not even Eurymas
        could fault . . .

26   And you too,
    O lord Apollo, strike the guilty ones
    with harm, destroy them as you do destroy,*
    but prosper us . . .

49   You most hateful . . .
        sneak-thief who roams about the town at night.

116   Let Paros go—those figs, that life at sea.

117   Sing, Muse, of the coiffeur Glaucus . . .

122 (*A father speaks*)
    There's nothing now you can't expect, nothing's
        against the odds,
    there are no miracles, now Zeus the father of the
        gods
    has turned the noonday into night and hidden the
        bright sun
    out of the sky, so clammy dread came over
        everyone.
    From now on all is credible, and like enough to be:
    let none of you now be surprised at anything you
        see,
    not even if land animals switch to where dolphins
        roam,
    and the salt sea and the crashing waves become
        their chosen home,
    while dolphins take a fancy to the mountains and
        the trees.

Indeed, already we observe that Archeanactides,
the . . . the son of . . .
has entered wedlock . . .
. . . but my daughter . . .

124 (*To Pericles*)
. . . like Mykonos people . . .
you drank my wine in quantity and strength
and brought no contribution . . .
and you didn't wait to be invited, like
a friend; your belly led your wits astray
to shamelessness . . .

125   I crave a fight with you, it's like a thirst.

126   But I do have one good skill,
that's to repay whoever hurts me with a
corresponding ill.

223   It's a cicada you've got by the wing.

127   So I did wrong. I daresay others have been caught
the same.

128   Heart, my heart, with helpless, sightless troubles
now confounded,
up, withstand the enemy, opposing breast to
breast.
All around they lie in wait, but stand you firmly
grounded,
not over-proud in victory, nor in defeat oppressed.
In your rejoicing let your joy, in hardship your
despairs
be tempered: understand the pattern shaping
men's affairs.

129   For now, my heart, your friends let you go hang.

130   It all depends upon the gods. Often enough, when
men
are prostrate on the ground with woe, they set
them up again;
and often enough, when men are standing proud
and all seems bright,
they tip them over on their backs, and then they're
in a plight—

a man goes wandering, short of bread, out of his
    mind with fright.

131–2 Mortals have moods that vary, Glaucus, son of
        Leptines,
      according to the kind of day that father Zeus
        decrees;
      their attitudes are governed by whatever each one
        sees.

133 No one here enjoys respect or reputation once he's
      dead:
    in this city we the living tend to cultivate instead
    the living's favour. Once you die, you get the
      worst of everything.

134 After all, it isn't good to mock the dead . . .

205   Otherwise
you'd not be using scent, a crone like you.

206 . . . fat round the ankles, a disgusting creature.

213 . . . with their lives in the arms of the waves.

215 (*On the loss at sea of the poet's sister's husband*)
        I feel no interest
in iambi or amusements.

216 Now I'll be called an auxiliary, like a Carian.

217 . . . with hair cut off the shoulders, basin-fashion.

220   In that event
I'd want the earth to open and swallow me.

233   In that situation
your legs are your best possession.

259 Not even Heracles beat two at once.

297 He was skulking at home, the revolting prat.

302   We often see
how wealth that was built up by much hard work
all drains away into a harlot's gut.

Adesp. 35
    . . . avenging spirits . . .
Be sure of this: the gods take awful toll
of impious men who wrong their dearest ones,

and no one who's betrayed his mother or
his sister's ever done well out of it.
You'll pay the price, I prophesy you will:
however many sheep you slaughter for
her wedding-feast, a fate implacable
will get you . . . you won't soften your heart
or . . . when you've ruined an innocent.
Even when gods are well-disposed, one can't
please them in everything . . .

Adesp. 38

　　　. . . His teeth were chattering . . .
As for running when you have to—as on that
　　　occasion God,
being angry with those people, drove the enemy
　　　army on—
that was no disgrace to you . . . my long-haired
　　　lad,
that you shook your sturdy shield off and turned
　　　tail . . . .
Braver men than you have given way to panics
　　　such as that;
nobody can beat the gods. But as for quitting the
　　　campaign
out of all the rest, and coming hotfoot back across
　　　the sea,
not a scratch upon you, well now, not much glory
　　　for you there.

Elegies

1　　I am a servant of the lord god of war,
　　　and one versed in the Muses' lovely gifts.

2　　On my spear's my daily bread,
　　　　on my spear my wine
　　from Ismaros;* and drinking it,
　　　　it's on my spear I recline.

3　　There won't be many bows drawn, nor much
　　　　　slingshot,
　　when on the plain the War-god brings the fight

together; it will be an agony
of swords—that is the warfare that the doughty
barons of Euboea are expert at . . .

4   But come now, take the cup and pass along
the clipper's benches, open up the casks
and draw the red wine off the lees—we too
shall need some drink to get us through this
    watch.

5   Some Saian* sports my splendid shield:
    I had to leave it in a wood,
but saved my skin. Well, I don't care—
    I'll get another just as good.

6   . . . giving the enemy
a nasty leaving-present . . .

14   Aisimides, if you mind what other folk
will say, you'll never have a lovely time.

15   Glaucus, an auxiliary's a buddy
for just so long as he's prepared to fight.

16   It's Luck and Destiny, Pericles, that bring
whatever a man gets . . .

17   Everything comes to men from work
and human effort . . .

9 (*On the loss at sea of the poet's sister's husband*)
It would have been less hard, if we had had
his head, his fair limbs to wrap up in white
for the holy fire to operate upon.

. . .

11   Well, wine will help . . .
For tears won't heal my wound; if I attend
feasts and diversions, they won't make it worse.

Further fragments on shipwrecks

8   And often in the reaches of the white-hair-tossing
    sea
they prayed for sweet safe homecoming . . .

12   . . . put lord Poseidon's painful offerings away . . .

13   Not a man in the town will find fault, Pericles,
       with our mourning, and enjoy his festival,
       nor in the canton: such fine men the surge
       of the tempestuous sea has overwhelmed,
       and swollen are our lungs with piercing pain.
          But then, my friend, the gods for ills past
                healing
       have set endurance as the antidote.
       This woe is different men's at different times:
       now it has come our way, and we bemoan
       our bleeding wound; another day 'twill pass
       to others. Come then, everyone endure,
       spend no more time in womanish lament.

SEMONIDES

1   Loud-thundering Zeus controls the outcome, lad,
     in everything, and makes it how he wants.
     Men have no foresight, but from day to day
     they live like cattle, knowing not at all
     how God will bring each matter to its end;
     yet everybody feeds on hope and trust
     throughout his vain endeavours. Some await
     tomorrow, some the turning of the seasons;
     there's no man does not think he'll reach next year
     the Wealth-god's darling, and society's.
     But one is overtaken by old age
     before he makes his goal, others succumb
     to grim diseases, others slain in war
     Hades escorts below dark earth, while some
     die out at sea, by tempests buffeted
     and the salt purple deep's unending waves,
     when they can make no living on the land;
     others again fasten themselves a noose
     and leave the sunlight by their own grim choice.
     So we are spared no ill, but numberless
     dangers and hurts for which we cannot plan
     exist for mortals. If I had my way,
     we would not cling to sorrow, or so long
     torment ourselves by dwelling on our woes.

2   When someone died, we would not think of him—
     if we had any sense—more than a day.

3   For we have time enough for being dead;
     for living, just a few unhappy years.

4   No life is wholly free from fault or harm.

5   . . . runs like an unweaned colt beside its dam.

6   A wife?* There's nothing better a man can get
     than a good one—and nothing ghastlier than a
           bad.

7   God made diverse the ways of womankind.
     One he created from a hairy sow;
     in her house everything's a mess of filth
     rolling about untidy on the floor,
     and she herself, unwashed, in dirty clothes,
     eats herself fat and wallows in the muck.

     One from a wicked vixen he created,
     expert in every trick. She misses nothing
     so long as it's bad, or even if it's good:
     what's good she mostly denigrates, what's bad
     she praises. But her moods are changeable.

     One from a bitch: a slut, that by herself
     gets pregnant; wants to hear and wants to know
     every damned thing, peers everywhere and prowls
     and yelps although there's no one to be seen.
     The man can't make her stop, neither with threats
     nor if he knocks her teeth out with a stone
     in rage, nor if he speaks with gentle words,
     not even if she's sitting among guests,
     but all the time he has this hopeless blight.

     Another the Olympians shaped from earth
     and gave a man: a lame duck, ignorant
     of good and ill alike. The only skill
     she knows is eating—oh, and when God sends
     a frost, to pull her chair up to the fire.

     Another from the sea: she has two moods.
     One day she sparkles and her face is bright;
     a guest who sees her will pay compliments,
     'No finer, fairer wife in all the world!'
     Another day she's insupportable
     to look at or go near to, raging mad
     like a bitch over her puppies, savagely
     at odds with friends and enemies alike—
     just as the sea sometimes stands motionless
     and harmless, a delight to those who sail,
     in summertime, but sometimes rages wild
     with thunderous swell rampaging to and fro.
     That's what this kind of woman's like—in mood,
     I mean; there's no resemblance in her looks!

     Another from an obstinate grey ass,

that after thwacks and curses just consents
and does the minimum. And then she eats
in the shadows, eats at the hearth, all night, all day;
and likewise hungry for the act of love
she welcomes anyone that comes along.

One from a weasel—miserable breed,
with no fair feature or desirable
or lovely or delightful to her name.
She's quite resourceless in the bed of love,
making the passenger seasick. She's a pest
to neighbours with her thieving; often, too,
she eats the food that was for sacrifice.

A fancy mare was mother to another,
who baulks at chores or anything that's hard
and wouldn't touch a millstone, lift a sieve,
or clear the shit out, or sit at the stove
for fear of soot; and yet compels a man
to love her. Twice a day she takes a bath,
or three times, some days; then she puts on scent.
Her long, lush hair is always combed, and decked
with flowers: hah, this sort of woman makes
a lovely sight for others, but a plague
for the man she belongs to, that's to say unless
he's some big tyrant or some sceptred king
whose heart takes pride in suchlike fripperies.

One from a monkey: quite the deadest loss
that Zeus has given us, this one. Ugly face—
the whole town sniggers when this sort goes past;
short in the neck; in all her movements stiff,
fixed legs, no bum. Poor sod, who cuddles that!
And like a monkey, she knows all the tricks
and tropes, oh yes, but doesn't like a joke.
She'd do no good to anyone, but looks
and thinks all day how she can do most harm.

One from a bee: he's lucky who gets her,
for she's the only one on whom no blame
alights. Wealth grows and prospers at her hands.
Bound in affection with her husband she
grows old, her children handsome and esteemed.
Among all women she stands out; a charm

divine surrounds her. She does not enjoy
sitting with women when they talk of sex.
Of all the wives that Zeus bestows on men,
this kind's the finest and most sensible.

But all those other breeds, by Zeus' design,
exist and ever will abide with men.
Yes, the worst pestilence Zeus ever made
is women. Even if they look to be
a helpmeet, yet the master suffers most:
the man who keeps a woman in his house
never gets through a whole day in good cheer,
nor will he soon drive Hunger from his door,
that hostile lodger, hateful deity.
When with his household he seems most content,
whether by God's grace or on man's account,
she finds some fault, and girds herself for war.
Where there's a woman, they may not be keen
even to welcome in a visitor.
I'll tell you, she that looks the best-behaved
in fact is the most rotten of them all,
for while her man gawps fondly at her, oh,
the neighbours' merriment: another dupe!

Yes, when the talk's of wives, each man will praise
his own and criticize the other bloke's,
but we don't realize it's equal shares.
For Zeus made wives as his worst pestilence
and fettered us in bonds unbreakable.
It's long been so: remember those who fought
round Troy's old city for a woman's sake
and found a home in Hades, [and again
those others who were murdered at their
        hearth . . .]

8   . . . like an eel down in the slime.

9   A heron, coming on a buzzard eating
       a fine Maeander eel, took it away.

10   Why do I make a lengthy tale of this?

10a   Do not be proud of never washing, nor
       a water-maniac; grow no bushy beard,
       nor wrap your body in a filthy cloak.

13   And then we had
that beetle flying up, which of all creatures
follows the most disgusting way of life.

14   A man who in the wooded mountains met
a lion or a leopard, all alone
on a narrow path, would not have been more
      scared.

15   To tunny squid's a meal, to gudgeon, shrimps.

16   . . . and rubbed myself with unguents and sweet
      scents
and myrrh, seeing among the company
a merchant or so.

17   And I squashed through the entrance at the rear.

18   . . . slouching along, his neck arched like a horse.

20   . . . sacrificing to the Nymphs
and Maia's son,* for they're of shepherd stock.

21*a*   . . . thrown out, weighed down
by their wet garments.

22–3   My word, Telembrotus, your preparations
are quite elaborate . . .
Now here's a wonderful Tromilian cheese
from Achaea, that I brought back . . .

24 (*A cook speaks*)
     . . . and how I roasted and cut up the pork
sacrifice-style—I'm not so bad at that.

25   But no one gave so much as a ladleful
of dregs.

26   He cleared away the table and the cups.

27   This one with a peaked rim's an Argive cup.

28   Its hind trotters were twitching.

30   . . . with the thighbones burnt.

31*a*   . . . the dry sticks are on the fire.

42   Gods easily give men the wrong idea.

CALLINUS

1   How long will you lie idle? When will you young
     men
    take courage? Don't our neighbours make you
     feel
ashamed, so much at ease? You look to sit at
    peace,
    but all the country's in the grip of war!
    .   .   .   .   .

    and throw your last spear even as you die.
For proud it is and precious for a man to fight
    defending country, children, wedded wife
against the foe. Death comes no sooner than the
    Fates
    have spun the thread; so charge, turn not aside,
with levelled spear and brave heart in behind the
    shield
    from the first moment that the armies meet.
A man has no escape from his appointed death,
    not though his blood be of immortal stock.
Men sometimes flee the carnage and the clattering
    of spears, and meet their destiny at home,
but such as these the people do not love or miss:
    the hero's fate is mourned by high and low.
Everyone feels the loss of the stout-hearted man
    who dies; alive, he ranks with demigods,
for in the people's eyes he is a tower of strength,
    his single efforts worth a company's.

2, 2a (*A prayer to Zeus*)
    Have mercy on us Smyrnaeans . . .
    Think of the times Smyrnaeans have for thee
    burned fine ox-thighbones.

5a, 4 And now the fierce Cimmerian horde* is on the
     march,
    with Trerians in its wake.

EUMELUS

696*   For the god of Ithome approves of the Muse
who comes unsullied and wearing the sandals of
freedom.

TYRTAEUS

2   . . . let us obey [the kings, who are]
        nearer the line [of the gods].
    For fair-crowned Hera's husband, Kronos' son
        himself,
      Zeus, gave the sons of Heracles this state.
    Under their lead we left windswept Erineos
        and came to Pelops' broad sea-circled land.*

4   This was the oracle from Phoebus that they heard
        at Delphi, and brought back the god's decree:
    'First in debate shall heaven's favourites, the kings,
        the guardians of fair Sparta's polity,
    speak, and the elders. After them the commoners
        shall to direct proposals make response
    with conscientious speech and all just
        consequence,
      making no twisted plans against our realm;
    and commoners' majority shall win the day.'
      Phoebus brought forth this guidance for the state.

5   . . . our sovereign Theopompus, whom the gods
        did love,
      through whom we took Messene's broad
        dance-grounds,
    Messene good to plough and good to plant for
        fruit.
      To conquer her they fought full nineteen years
    steadfastly ever, with endurance in their hearts,
        those spearmen of our fathers' fathers' time,
    and in the twentieth the foe took flight, and left
        their fertile farms among Ithome's heights.

6 (*The enslaved Messenians were*)
        like donkeys suffering under heavy loads,
      by painful force compelled to bring their masters
        half
        of all the produce that the soil brought forth.

7   . . . making a wailing funeral chorus, they and
        their wives,
    when one of their masters met his destiny.

10   For it is fine to die in the front line,
     a brave man fighting for his fatherland,
and the most painful fate's to leave one's town
     and fertile farmlands for a beggar's life,
roaming with mother dear and aged father,
     with little children and with wedded wife.
He'll not be welcome anywhere he goes,
     bowing to need and horrid poverty,
his line disgraced, his handsome face belied;
     every humiliation dogs his steps.
This is the truth: the vagrant is ignored
     and slighted, and his children after him.
So let us fight with spirit for our land,
     die for our sons, and spare our lives no more.
You young men, keep together, hold the line,
     do not start panic or disgraceful rout.
Keep grand and valiant spirits in your hearts,
     be not in love with life—the fight's with men!
Do not desert your elders, men with legs
     no longer nimble, by recourse to flight:
it is disgraceful when an older man
     falls in the front line while the young hold back,
with head already white, and grizzled beard,
     gasping his valiant breath out in the dust
and clutching at his bloodied genitals,
     his nakedness exposed: a shameful sight
and scandalous. But for the young man, still
     in glorious prime, it is all beautiful:
alive, he draws men's eyes and women's hearts;
     felled in the front line, he is lovely yet.
Let every man then, feet set firm apart,
     bite on his lip and stand against the foe.

11   But Heracles unvanquished sowed your stock:
     take heart! Zeus bows not yet beneath the yoke.
Fear not the throng of men, turn not to flight,
     but straight toward the front line bear your
       shields,

despising life and welcoming the dark
  contingencies of death like shafts of sun.
You know what wreck the woeful War-god makes,
  and are well to the grim fight's temper tuned.
You have been with pursuers and pursued,
  you young men, and had bellyful of both.
You know that those who bravely hold the line
  and press toward engagement at the front
die in less numbers, with the ranks behind
  protected; those who run, lose all esteem.
The list is endless of the ills that hurt
  the man who learns to think the coward's
      thoughts:
for it's a bad place, as he flees the fray,
  to have his wound, between the shoulder-blades,
and it's a shameful sight to see him lie
  dead in the dust, the spear-point in his back.
Let every man, then, feet set firm apart,
  bite on his lip and stand against the foe,
his thighs and shins, his shoulders and his chest
  all hidden by the broad bulge of his shield.
Let his right hand brandish the savage lance,
  the plume nod fearsomely above his head.
By fierce deeds let him teach himself to fight,
  and not stand out of fire—he has a shield—
but get in close, engage, and stab with lance
  or sword, and strike his adversary down.
Plant foot by foeman's foot, press shield on shield,
  thrust helm at helm, and tangle plume with
      plume,
opposing breast to breast: that's how to fight,
  with the long lance or sword-grip in your hand.
You light-armed men, wherever you can aim
  from the shield-cover, pelt them with great rocks
and hurl at them your smooth-shaved javelins,
  helping the armoured troops with close support.

12   I would not rate a man worth mention or account
       either for speed of foot or wrestling skill,
     not even if he had a Cyclops' size and strength
       or could outrun the fierce north wind of Thrace;

I would not care if he surpassed Tithonus' looks,
  or Cinyras' or Midas' famous wealth,
or were more royal than Pelops son of Tantalus,
  or had Adrastus' smooth persuasive tongue,
or fame for everything save only valour: no,
  no man's of high regard in time of war
unless he can endure the sight of blood and death,
  and stand close to the enemy, and fight.
This is the highest worth, the finest human prize
  and fairest for a bold young man to win.
It benefits the whole community and state,
  when with a firm stance in the foremost rank
a man bides steadfast, with no thought of shameful
    flight,
  laying his life and stout heart on the line,
and standing by the next man speaks
    encouragement.
  This is the man of worth in time of war.
Soon he turns back the foemen's sharp-edged
    battle lines
  and strenuously stems the tide of arms;
his own dear life he loses, in the front line felled,
  his breast, his bossed shield pierced by many a
    wound,
and of his corselet all the front, but he has brought
  glory upon his father, army, town.
His death is mourned alike by young and old; the
    whole
  community feels the keen loss its own.
People point out his tomb, his children in the
    street,
  his children's children and posterity.
His name and glorious reputation never die;
  he is immortal even in his grave,
that man the furious War-god kills as he defends
  his soil and children with heroic stand.
Or if in winning his proud spear-vaunt he escapes
  the doom of death and grief's long shadow-cast,
then all men do him honour, young and old alike;
  much joy is his before he goes below.

He grows old in celebrity, and no one thinks
  to cheat him of his due respect and rights,
but all men at the public seats make room for him,
  the young, the old, and those of his own age.
This is the excellence whose heights one now must seek
  to scale, by not relenting in the fight.

13   . . . a tawny lion's spirit in your breast.

14   . . . until it ends
  in highest heroism, or in death.

19   . . . throwers of stones, and archers,
  . . . like hordes of wasps . . .
  . . . the man-destroying War-god . . .

  . . . protected by your convex shields,
Pamphyloi, Hylleis, and Dymanes,* each distinct,
  your murderous lances levelled in your hands.
. . . (not?) leave it all to the immortal gods

but with concerted charge at once we'll crush their
    front,
  meeting the enemy spearmen face to face.
A fearsome clangour will be heard, as the two sides
  dash shields against round shields . . .
          . . . falling upon each other,
  and corselets on men's breasts will fend away
destruction, yet be dented by the points of spears.
  The brazen helmets will resound beneath
the battering of rocks . . .

23a   But as they fight, Athena, pale-eyed daughter
of Zeus who holds the Aegis,* checks the wild
     spears' flight.
  A multitude will throw with javelins
sharp-pointed . . .
  in light arms running forward . . .
Arcadians . . . the Argives' . . . along the wall . . .
  . . . from pale-eyed Athena . . . ditch . . .
They will kill every Spartan that they catch
  fleeing the battle . . .

MIMNERMUS

1   What's life, what's joy, without love's heavenly
        gold?
    I hope I die when I no longer care
    for secret closeness, tender favours, bed,
        which are the rapturous flowers that grace
            youth's prime
    for men and women. But when painful age
        comes on, that makes a man loathsome and vile,
    malignant troubles ever vex his heart;
        seeing the sunlight gives him joy no more.
    He is abhorred by boys, by women scorned:
        so hard a thing God made old age to be.

2   But we are like the leaves that flowery spring
        puts forth, quick spreading in the sun's warm light:
    for a brief span of time we take our joy
        in our youth's bloom, the future, good or ill,
    kept from us, while the twin dark Dooms stand by,
        one bringing to fulfilment harsh old age,
    the other, death. The ripeness of youth's fruit
        is short, short as the sunlight on the earth,
    and once this season of perfection's past,
        it's better to be dead than stay alive.
    All kinds of worry come. One man's estate
        is failing, and there's painful poverty;
    another has no sons—the keenest need
        one feels as one goes down below the earth;
    sickness wears down another's heart. There's none
        Zeus does not give a multitude of ills.

3   Most handsome once, perhaps, but when his
        season's past,
    he's loathed and slighted even by his sons.

4   He gave Tithonus* an unending bane,
        old age, that is more frightful than harsh death.

5   The sweat runs down me, and my heart's a-flutter,
        seeing my generation in its bloom

of joy and beauty. Oh, it ought to last
   for longer! But it's fleeting as a dream,
our precious youth; in no time ugly, harsh,
   hateful old age is looming over us,
unvalued, that enveloping deforms
   past recognition, dims both sight and mind.

6   I pray my fated death may catch me
       hale and hearty at threescore years.

7   Enjoy yourself. As for the wretched townsfolk,
       some will speak ill of you—but only some.

8   Let us be honest, you and me.
       It is the rightest thing to be.

9   Aipy we left,* and Neleus' city, Pylos,
       and came by ship to Asia's lovely coast.
    We settled at fair Colophon with rude
       aggression, bringers of harsh insolence;
    from there we crossed the river Asteïs (?)
       and took Aeolian Smyrna by God's will.

11, 11*a*

Jason would not have brought that great fleece* home
    from Aea at the end of that ordeal
he suffered for the arrogant Pelias;
    they'd not have reached the river of World's End.

      .   .   .   .   .

Aeetes' city, where the swift sun's rays
    are stored in a gold chamber by the edge
of the world stream, where godlike Jason went.

12   The sun must toil along day after day:
       there's never any break or rest for him
    or for his horses, once rosefinger Dawn
       leaves the world stream and climbs into the sky.
    A wondrous couch bears him across the waves—
       winged, by Hephaestus intricately wrought
    in precious gold—as he in grateful sleep
       skims o'er the sea from the Hesperides
    to Aethiopia,* where a chariot
       and steeds await the early birth of Dawn;
    and there the god mounts his new equipage,
       Hyperion's son.

13*a*   So when the king had given his command,
            they charged, protected by their convex shields.

14   His strength and bravery were not like yours,
            as I have heard from older men who saw
        him on the plain of Hermos* with his spear
            routing the Lydian cavalry's thick ranks.
        Pallas Athena ne'er had cause to fault
            his acid fury, when in the front line
        he hurtled through the battle's bloody moil
            against the stinging missiles of the foe.
        No warrior of the enemy remained
            his better in the strenuous work of war,
        so long as he moved in the swift sun's light.

Seventh to Sixth Century

ALCMAN

1   ... Among the dead, Lykaithos concerns me not,*
nor Enarsphoros and fleet-foot Sebros
and the mighty ... and the warrior ...,
Euteiches, lord Areitos, and ...
outstanding among the heroes of old ...
great Eurytos ... the nobles;
all these we shall pass by:
Measure and Means* are senior of the gods,
and help from Zeus comes prompt, nor waits
to do up shoes. Let no man seek to fly
to heaven, possess in love
fair Aphrodite, or the queen of gods,
or some delicious nymph;
but the sweet-eyed Graces of music may go in
to the hall of Zeus.

             .   .   .

One was slain with an arrow, one laid low
with a bright millstone ... Hades ...
So they paid dearly for their wickedness.

There's such a thing
as God's requital. Fortunate is he
who in good heart plaits up his day sans tears.
Now my song's of the radiance
of Agido: she to my eyes
shines like the sun she calls to be our witness.
But I must not speak good or ill of her
when the dancers' famous principal herself
stands out like a racehorse set among the sheep,
a thundering winner, the sort you see in dreams
as you doze in a cavern's shade.

Ah, look—the mount's a Venetian;*
that combed-out hair
of cousin Hagesichora has a sheen
like purest gold,
and that silver face—why say it in words?
There's Hagesichora;
while Agido's nearest challenger for looks
will be a Scythian nag to an Ibenian.
The Pleiades that go up before daybreak
fight it out with us as we bear
the plough,* our Sirius, through the ambrosial
     night.

Our purple finery is not
the treasure that defends us,
no coiled snake-bangle of solid gold,
nor Lydian headband splendid upon girls
with big dark eyes,
nor Nanno's hair, no, nor nymphlike Areta,
nor Thulakis, nor Klesithera; nor
will you go to Ainesimbrota's* and say
'Oh please make Astaphis mine'
or 'Make Philylla look my way',
Damareta, or sweet Vianthemis.
No, it's Hagesichora—
she is my heartache.

For her beauty of ankles is not here in the dance:
she bides by Agido, commends
our ceremonial. Gods, receive their prayers—
in the gods' hands lies fulfilment.
Dance-leader, I may say that in myself
I'm just a maid that vainly hoots
like the owl in the roof: Aotis* is the one
I chiefly hope to please,
who gives us relief from toil; but Hagesichora
brings girls into sweet concord.

For the team must turn with the trace-horse,
and the helmsman rules the ship.
The Sirens' tone indeed
is music more than ours;

they are divine, and not eleven girls
but ten sing in this choir. Yet it gives voice
like the swan on the waters of Xanthos,
and she with her darling flaxen hair,
Hagesichora . . .

2   There, in highest respect from gods and men,
they dwell . . . in a chamber divinely built,
masters of swift colts—Castor—
skilled horsemen—and glorious Polydeuces.

3   Muses of Olympus, my heart is rapt
with desire of hearing a new song
and the unison of girls in lovely melody
. . . will dispel
the sweetness of sleepy eyelids.
. . . draws me along to the piazza,
there where I'll be tossing my flaxen hair
. . . a dance for tender feet . . .

and with crippling longing. Her glance
more melting than sleep or death;
hers is a potent sweetness.

But Astymeloisa gives me no response,
just flits with her garland
like a falling star through the splendour of the night,
a golden shoot, a tuft of down—
gone in a few strides of her long legs.
All Cinyras' glistening charm
sits on our damsel hair,

But as to milady Astymeloisa,*
out in the crowd, she wins the public's heart.

If she would just come up, take my young hand,
I'd soon be begging her favour.

But as things are, in angry mood . . .
. . . the girl . . .

14(a) Hey Muse, euphonious Muse, full of melodies,
ever the singer,
make start of a new song for the girls to sing!

16   He was no yokel,
      no fool even among experts;
      not of Thessalian stock,
      no shepherd from Nether Wallop,
      but from the centre of Sardis.

17   And sometime I'll lend you a full-bellied cauldron
      in which you can put all your oddments together.
      It's never yet been on the fire, but soon it'll
      stand full of soup, the sort Alcman the trencherman
      dotes on, all hot in the depths of midwinter.
      For really, he doesn't eat anything fancy,
      but looks for the ordinary, just like the people.

19   Seven couches, and to each a table
      bedecked with poppy-seed rolls,
      linseed and sesame, and bowls
      of . . . stuck with golden honey.

20   Of seasons he created three,
      summer, winter, and autumn to boot;
      and for a fourth, the spring, when things
      are growing, but a man can't eat his fill.

26   My legs can support me no longer, young ladies
          with voices of honey and song divine!
      Ah, would that I could be a kingfisher, flying
      sea-blue, fearless, amid you halcyons
          down to rest on the foaming brine!

27   Hey Muse, daughter of Zeus, Calliope,
      make me a start of delightful poetry:
      give my song charm, and beautiful dancing.

38   And all the young girls among us
      speak highly of the man that plays the lyre.

39, 40 These verses and melody Alcman
      found by harking to the voice
      of chattering partridges . . .
      I know the tunes of all the birds.

45   May our chorus be pleasing to all Zeus' house
      and to thee, lord Apollo.

56   Often enough, in the heights of the mountains
      when festival torches pleasure the gods,

you've taken a golden bowl, a big one
like shepherds have; filled it with milk of a lioness,
then made a big firm cheese for Hermes slayer of
    Argus.*

58   It's not the goddess of love,
just wild Cupid playing his boyish games,
alighting on the petals—please don't touch!—
of my galingale garland.

59a   Cupid once more by the goddess's grace
trickles down in his sweetness, warming my heart.

59b   Such is the offering of pleasant Muses
made manifest by Megalostrata
the flaxen-haired, a girl for girls to envy.

60   'And I pray to you, bringing this garland
of helichryse and lovely galingale.'

81   And the girls all say,
'Father Zeus, I wish he could be *my* husband!'

89   They sleep, the mountain peaks,
the clefts, ridges, and gullies,
and all the creatures that the dark earth feeds,
the animals of the glen, the tribe of bees,
the monsters of the salt purple deeps.
They sleep, the tribes
of winging birds . . .

96   Soon he'll be serving bean-pottage,
white groats, and the fruit of the honeycomb.

98   At feasts and at men's mess unions
with banqueters gathered it's fitting to start on the
    paean.

P. Oxy. 2443 fr. 1 +3213
    . . . as I went up from Trygeai
to the White Goddesses' beautiful precinct
with two sweet pomegranates.
The girls, having prayed to the fair-flowing river
for lovely fulfilment of marriage
and the supreme experience
that men and women know, the bridal bed,

    .   .   .

SAPPHO

1   Rich-throned immortal Aphrodite,
       scheming daughter of Zeus, I pray you,
with pain and sickness, Queen, crush not my
       heart,

     but come, if ever in the past you
       heard my voice from afar and hearkened,
and left your father's halls and came, with gold

     chariot yoked; and pretty sparrows
       brought you swiftly across the dark earth
fluttering wings from heaven through the air.

     Soon they were here, and you, Blest Goddess,
       smiling with your immortal features,
asked why I'd called, what was the matter now,

     what was my heart insanely craving:
       'Who is it this time I must cozen
to love you, Sappho? Who's unfair to you?

     'For though she flee, soon she'll be chasing;
       though she refuse gifts, she'll be giving;
though she love not, she'll love despite herself.'

     Yes, come once more, from sore obsession
       free me; all that my heart desires
fulfilled, fulfil—help me to victory!

2   Come, goddess, to your holy shrine,
       where your delightful apple grove
awaits, and altars smoke with frankincense.

     A cool brook sounds through apple boughs,
       and all's with roses overhung;
from shimmering leaves a trancelike sleep takes
       hold.

     Here is a flowery meadow, too,
       where horses graze, and gentle blow
the breezes . . .

Here, then, Love-goddess much in mind,
      infuse our feast in gracious style
with nectar poured in cups that turn to gold.

5   Love-goddess and Sea-nymphs, please let
      my brother reach here safe and sound,
and all his heart's desires be fulfilled,

      but let him undo all his past
      mistakes, gladden his friends and vex
his enemies, and . . .

      May he be ready to respect
      his sister, and from hurtful pains

          .   .   .   .

15   . . . Love-goddess; may he find you harsh,
      and Doricha* not boast again
of how his longing's brought him back to her.

16   Some think a fleet, a troop of horse
      or soldiery the finest sight
in all the world; but I say, what one loves.

      Easy it is to make this plain
      to anyone. She the most fair
of mortals, Helen, having a man of the best,

      deserted him, and sailed to Troy,
      without a thought for her dear child
or parents, led astray by [love's power.]

      [For though the heart be pr]oud [and strong,]
      [Love] quickly [bends it to his will. —]
That makes me think of Anactoria.

      I'd sooner see her lovely walk
      and the bright sparkling of her face
than all the horse and arms of Lydia.

17   O lady Hera, may my prayer
      bring thy enchanting presence close,
that Atreus' royal sons* established here

      when they had gone through many trials,
      round Ilios first, and then at sea:
when they came here they could not journey on

before invoking thee, and Zeus
of Suppliants, and Thyone's son*
the lovely. Now grant me thy ancient grace.

Holy and fair . . . virg . . .

22   . . . take the soft harp,
Abanthis, sing of Gongyla;
that yearning aura's on you once again,

my dear. It thrilled you, didn't it,
seeing that dress of hers? I'm glad.
The Love-goddess herself has chided me

for praying [for new sweethearts and
forgetting old ones] . . .

23   . . . love . . .

For when I see you face to face,
I think, was even Hermione*
so fair? Helen herself, perhaps, if so

a mortal may be praised. Know this:
your kindness would be my release
from all my brooding . . .

24   Why, we too did all that when we were young.
Yes, lovely times we . . .

30   . . . and girls
in nightlong celebration sing
of you and of your flower-bosomed bride.

So wake, and go to join your friends,
the lads. I reckon we shall see
less sleep than the melodious nightingale.

31   He looks to me to be in heaven,
that man who sits across from you
and listens near you to your soft speaking,

your laughing lovely: that, I vow,
makes the heart leap in my breast;
for watching you a moment, speech fails me,

my tongue is paralysed, at once
a light fire runs beneath my skin,
my eyes are blinded, and my ears drumming,

the sweat pours down me, and I shake
all over, sallower than grass:
I feel as if I'm not far off dying.

But no thing is too hard to bear;
for [God can make] the poor man [rich,
or bring to nothing heaven-high fortune.]

32 (*The Muses*)

who gave me of their craft, and so
set me in high regard.

33   O Aphrodite, crowned in gold,
if only I could have such luck!

34   The stars about the lovely moon
withdraw and hide their shining forms,
when at her full she bathes the earth in light
. . . silver . . .

36   . . . and I yearn, and I desire . . .

39   A decorated slipper hid
her foot, a lovely piece of Lydian work.

41   I cannot change my mind for you, my dears.

44   So the herald Idaeus arrived with the message
swift.
'. . . glory that never fades.
Hector comes with his company, bringing from
holy Thebes*
and from Plakos' perennial fountain a lovely bride,
rich Andromache, voyaging over the briny sea.
Countless bangles of gold they are bringing, and
crimson-dyed
robes that float with the breezes, and ornaments
finely made,
drinking-vessels of silver past number, and ivory.'
Hector's father sprang eagerly up when he heard
the news,
word soon came to the friends of the family
through the town:
Ilus' noble descendants* got busy and harnessed
mules

to their finely built carriages; all of the wives got
    in,
all the girls with their delicate ankles, and on their
    own
Priam's daughters . . .
while the bachelors harnessed their horses to
    chariots
                              . . . to Ilios.
Lyres, melodious shawms, and the clatter of
    castanets
blended there, and the voices of girls in the holy
    song;
up to heaven the glorious clamour arose . . .
Everywhere in the streets there were bowls full of
    wine, and cups,
myrrh and cassia, frankincense, fragrances all
    pell-mell.
All the women of matronly age shouted Eleleu!
while the men singing out in the beautiful
    Steepscale Hymn
called on Paeon, the god of the excellent bow and
    lyre,
praising Hector the prince and Andromache his
    princess.

44A   Phoebus golden of hair, whom the daughter of
          Koios* bore
after union with Zeus son of Kronos, whose name
    is great.
In Zeus' presence then Artemis swore with the
    gods' great oath:
'By thy head, I will keep myself virgin for evermore,
roaming free in the heights of the mountains, the
    lonely peaks.
Nod now, grant me this favour!' she said, and the
    blessed gods'
father nodded, confirming it. Therefore do gods
    and men
call her virgin and deershooter, goddess of all the
    wild;
noble titles; and Eros can never go near to her . . .

46   . . . while I
    on soft cushions will spread . . .

47   Love
    shakes my heart like the wind rushing down on
        the mountain oaks.

48   You came, and I needed you,
    and you cooled the fever of longing that racked my
        heart.

49   Love? Why, I was in love with you, Atthis, a long
        time back.
    Just a plain little girl to my eyes, but . . .

50   For the beautiful person is beautiful just in form,
    but the noble of soul will soon seem to have
        beauty too.

51   I'm uncertain now what I should do; I am in two
        minds.

52   I don't reckon to reach to the sky.

53   Holy spirits of Joy, rosy of arm, daughters of Zeus,
        come nigh.

54   Eros, coming from heaven wrapped in a crimson
        cloak.

55 (*To a wealthy but unmusical lady*)
    Yes, and when you are dead, there you will lie for
        aye
    unremembered, because none of Pieria's
    roses* touch you, but unnoticed in Hades too
    you will hover among faded forgotten ghosts.

56   As to musical skill, never, I think, again
    shall we see such a girl born to the light of day.

57 (*To Andromeda*)
    Who's this country colleen casting a spell on you,
    one who hasn't yet learned how to arrange her
        shift
    well down over her calves?

58   . . . young girls . . .
    . . . deep-bosomed Muses' lovely gifts
    . . . clear melodious lyre.

But as for me, old age has got my whole
body, my hair is white that once was dark.
. . . my knees will not hold up
. . . to dance like the young fawns
. . . but what can I do?
To stay untouched by age, that cannot be:
a lesson, so they say, the goddess Dawn
learned, when in her rose arms she bore Tithonus
off to the world's east limit; still old age
caught up with him . . . his immortal bride.

.   .   .   .   .   .

My liking's for the gracious. Thus does love
define my sunlight and my beautiful.

81   So set beautiful wreaths, Dika, about your tresses,
plait together the dill shoots with your tender
            fingers.
Primed with flowers, the blest spirits of Joy most
            favour
such occasions: they shun people who wear no
            garlands.

82   Mnasidika is shapelier
than tender Gyrinno.

94   .   .   .   .

Honestly, I wish I were dead.
She was covered in tears as she went away,

        left me, saying 'Oh, it's too bad!
        How unlucky we are! I swear,
Sappho, I don't want to be leaving you.'

        This is what I replied to her:
        'Go, be happy, and think of me.
You remember how we looked after you;
        or if not, then let me remind

                .   .   .   .   .

all the lovely and beautiful times we had,
        all the garlands of violets
        and of roses and . . .
and . . . that you've put on in my company,

all the delicate chains of flowers
that encircled your tender neck

.   .   .   .   .

and the costly unguent with which
you anointed yourself, and the royal myrrh.

On soft couches . . .
tender . . .
you assuaged your longing . . .

There was never a . . .
or a shrine or a . . .
. . . that we were not present at,

no grove . . . no festive dance . . .

95   I said 'Master, . . .
For by the blest lady . . .
I take no joy in walking under heaven,

but feel a strange desire to die
and see the dewy lotus-banks
of Acheron . . . .'

96   . . . she worshipped you
and always in your singing she most delighted.

But now among the women of Lydia
she shines, as after the sun has set
the rosy-fingered moon will appear, surpassing

all the stars, bestowing her light alike
upon the waves of the briny sea
and on the fields that sparkle with countless
        flowers.

Everything is bathed in the lovely dew:
roses take their nourishment, and
soft chervil, and the blossoming honey-lotus.

Often, as she moves on her daily round,
she'll be eating her tender heart
when she thinks of her love for gentle Atthis.

And for us to go there . . .
. . . it's not possible . . .
with the wedding-song(?) ringing loud between us.

For us to match the beauty of goddesses
is not easy . . .

98 (*To Sappho's daughter Cleïs*)

Why now, Cleïs your grandmother used to say

that when *she* was young, if they had
crimson ribbons to bind their hair,
that was quite an exceptional ornament.

But when someone has hair like yours
flaming brighter than any torch,
then it's very much nicer to have it so,

neatly garlanded with some fresh
blooming flowers. But as for these
broidered headbands, it's only just recently

that they've brought them from Sardis here
to the towns of Ionia

.   .   .   .   .   .

But I haven't the means to buy
such a headband for you, my dear.
Be content with our own Mytilenian . . .

99a   . . . of Polyanax's line
. . . Samian . . .

to strum across
the plectrum-welcoming strings . . .
. . . kindly
. . . and it vibrates harmoniously,

[while her fair v]oice
through the h[igh notes . . .

99b   O son of Zeus and Leto,*
come to the ceremony . . .
leave Gryneia's woods
and thy famed oracle

.   .   .   .   .   .

Again, it's the wild son
of Polyanax's line I want to expose.

101 (*To Aphrodite*)
> kerchieves and crimson-dyed
> aprons that float with the breeze
> . . . sent from Phocaea,
> precious gifts . . .

102   Darling mother, I can no longer ply my loom:
> I'm overcome with longing for a slender lad.

104*ab*   Hesperus, loveliest of all the stars . . .
> bringing back all that glowing Dawn sent forth:
> you bring the sheep,
> you bring the goat,
> you bring the girl to a home away from her mother.

105*a* (*On a girl*)
> Like the sweet-apple that's gleaming red on the
>   topmost bough,
> right at the very end, that the apple-pickers forgot,
> or rather didn't forget, but were just unable to
>   reach.

105*b*   Like the hyacinth on the hills that the passing
>   shepherds
> trample under their feet, and the purple bloom on
>   the ground . . .

106   supreme, like the singer from Lesbos performing
> abroad.

107   I still do cleave to maidenhood.

108 (*To a bride*)
> O you beauty, you charmer . . .

109   'We'll give her', says the father.

110   The doorman's feet* are size 90:
> five cowhides went into his sandals,
> and it took ten cobblers to make them!

111   High must be the chamber—
>   Hymenaeum!
> Make it high, you builders!
>
> A bridegroom's coming—
>   Hymenaeum!
> like the War-god himself, the tallest of the tall!

112   Happy groom, the union you prayed for
is now fulfilled, you have the girl of your prayers.
How handsome you are, with your gentle eyes,
and your lovely face all radiant with desire.
The Love-goddess has shown you special
       favour.

113   No other girl now, dear groom, like her . . .

114   'Maidenhood, my maidenhood,
      where are you going now?'
'I'll visit you no more, my dear,
      I'll visit you no more.'

115   To what, dear groom, can I best liken you?
To a slender sapling I most liken you.

116   Hail to the bride, all hail the honoured groom!

117   Good wishes, bride! Good wishes to the groom!

118   Come, noble lyre, take voice
and tell me . . .

120   But I am not the resentful sort.
      I have a placid heart.

121   No, be our friend, but take
a younger woman for your bed.
At my age I can't bring myself
to live with you.

122   I saw her picking flowers,
a girl exceeding tender . . .

123   Gold-sandalled Dawn has just . . .

126   Sleeping on her tender companion's bosom.

127   Muses, once more come nigh,
leave the gold halls of Zeus.

128   Come now, gracious spirits of Joy
      and Muses with lovely hair.

129*a*   And you have no thought of me.

129*b*   Or you love some other person more than me.

130   Once more I feel the sting of crippling Love,
that bittersweet, unmanageable midge.

Atthis, you've come to hate the thought of me,
you fly to join Andromeda.

132   I have a pretty child, like flowers
of gold her form, my precious Cleïs;
whom I would not exchange
for all of Lydia, or the lovely land . . .

133   Andromeda is well repaid.

. . . . .

Sappho, why do you . . . Aphrodite
who holds all fortune in her hands?

134   I dreamed I spoke with the Cyprian goddess.*

135   Why must the swallow wake me so soon, Eirana?

136   The nightingale that brings the news of spring
with lovely voice.

137 (*He*) 'There's something I want to say to you,
but I'm too shy . . . '

   (*She*) 'But if you wanted something good,
your tongue not brewing wicked words,
you'd not be shy, you'd speak as you saw fit.'

138   Stand facing me, dear man,
and let the beauty of your eyes shine out.

140   'Aphrodite, tender Adonis
is dying!* What can we do?'

'You must beat your breasts, o maidens,
you must tear your tunics too.'

141   There stood a bowl
of ambrosia mixed,
and Hermes took a jug and served the gods.

Then they all poured
libations from
their goblets, praying blessings on the groom.

142   Leto and Niobe* were the best of friends.

166   They say that Leda once did find an egg*
well covered in a clump of hyacinth.

143   And chick-peas grew there golden on the banks.

146   I'll do without the honey, and the stings.

147   I'm sure that people will remember us.

148   Wealth without class is no safe house-guest.

150 (*To her daughter*)
      In a house of the Muses' servants it's not right
      for there to be lament . . . it would not befit us.

154   The moon was shining full; about
          the altar they took their stand.

155   To the daughter of Polyanax's house
      most courteous greeting.

156   (she) more melodious than a harp,
      more gold than gold.

158   When anger's spreading through your breast,
      it's best to keep your yapping tongue in check.

160   Of these things I now
      make lovely song for pleasure of my friends.

ALCAEUS OR SAPPHO

1   I'll see my poor suffering homeland.

4   So, all-surveying Sun, I pray . . .

10   They cowered like birds at a swift
eagle suddenly seen.

16   Once Cretan girls used to dance
harmoniously like this,
soft-footed about the fair
altar . . . .
they made for the tender grass.

21*a*   A lad like this came riding into Thebes.

21*b*   Malis was spinning, a fine thread on her spindle.

23 (*Temptation?*)
gold-gleaming servant of Aphrodite.

25   And I'm on wings, like a child after its mother.

25B   Perdition that never has its fill.

35   . . . women
. . . breezes blowing
. . . to dance, lovely Abanthis.

42   . . . scheming Cyprian goddess . . .
. . . messenger from Zeus . . .
. . . come to Makar's island*
. . . solemn oath . . .

ALCAEUS

Hymns

34
From Pelops' sea-girt land come nigh,
great sons of Leda and of Zeus,
Castor and Pollux; O consent, appear,

ye who ride over all the earth
and the broad sea on swift-legg'd steeds
and rescue men with ease from chilly death,

leaping in brightness from afar
upon firm-thwarted vessels' masts,
on stormy watches bringing the dark ship light.

45
O Hebrus, loveliest of all
rivers, that gurgling through Thrace
comes out at Aenus to the purple sea,

where crowds of girls with tender hands
scoop you to sluice their pretty thighs,
water divine that kisses them like balm.

307
O lord Apollo, child of mighty Zeus

. . . . . .

Castalia, Tritaia's pride.

308 (*To Hermes*)
Hail, sovereign of Cyllene: thee
I fain would sing, whom Maia bore
when Kronos' son, the king of all,
made love to her amid the mountain peaks.

309 (*To the Muses?*)
For, with the gods' grace, that
will bring reward that never fades
to those who have you as their guardians.

325
O queen Athena, battle-tried,
who . . . by Coronea's . . .
before thy shrine, about [the altar,]
on the Coralius river's banks.

327 (*To Eros*)

>most formidable god,
>whom fair-shod Iris bore in love
>with gold-haired Zephyrus.

386   The holy Graces took you to their bosoms
from Kronos.

349   (*To Dionysus*)

(*Hera threw Hephaestus out of heaven. In retaliation he sent her a throne with a hidden trap inside it,*)

>so that none of the gods possibly could free her
>without his help.

(*She sat on it and was caught fast,*)

>and the immortal gods
>all were laughing . . .

>Ares declares he can
bring Hephaestus by force.

(*But he failed. Finally Dionysus overcame Hephaestus with drink and induced him to release his mother, who in gratitude persuaded the gods to admit Dionysus to Olympus as*)

>one of the Twelve.

Political songs

War with Athens

112   For fighting men are a town's battlements.

400   For death in battle is a splendid thing.

401B   Give Melanippus the message at home:
'Alcaeus is safe, but his fine armour and shield
the Athenians have hung up in the shrine
of the pale-eyed goddess.'

382 (*To Athena?*)

>or somewhere reunite
>the scattered army and inspire
>discipline in them.

Breach with Pittacus

71   You were a friend fit to invite to share
kid's meat or pork, as the convention is.

72   and wildly . . .
        fills with neat wine that's never still
by day or night . . .

        Well, once that fellow made his coup,
        he didn't give such habits up.
        He made disturbance every night;
cask after cask rang hollow to the foot.

        With such a mother, then, do you
        claim the esteem that free men have,
        from worthy parents born?

331   Melanchrus now deserves respect,
        . . . to the town

305a1   . . . Even if you leave that clan,
        the brew you've mixed . . .

(*Trying to reconcile us*)

        will be like trying to drain the foaming brine.

Myrsilus

305a2   Between us two may no dispute arise,
        nor . . .
        If anyone wants to divide us, Mnemon . . .

208   I can't make out the lie of the winds.
        One wave rolls up from one side, one
        from t'other; we between them toss
in our dark vessel, struggling against

        a furious storm. We've water shipped
        above the mast-box; you can see
        all through the sail, it's torn across,
the stays are working slack, the rudder's gone.

        . . . Both legs
stay tangled in the ropes—it's only this

        keeps me from being washed away:
        the cargo, walloped off the deck,
        floats overhead . . .

6   This wave is higher than the first:
         we'll have a job to bale it out
       if once it comes aboard . . .

Let's quickly batten down and run to port.

         Let none be soft or slow to move:
         the trials ahead are plain to see.
       Remember last time! Every man be true,

         let us not shamefully disgrace
         our worthy fathers in their graves,
       who . . . this town . . .

         Let us not bow to one man's rule,
         and let us not accept . . .

73   . . . every piece of freight
         . . . hugely in the swell.

         Buffeted now by wave on wave
         she says she has no heart . . .
       to fight the pouring rain, and so
       smashed on the unmarked rocks she comes to
             grief.

         Well, that's her lot, and here I'm stuck.
         I'll think no more of getting back,
         I'll just enjoy myself with you,
       and . . . with Bycchis . . .

         So even though . . .
         we for the day to come . . .

306 (i) . . . much sand . . .
         the eczema creeps up, it's spread
       right through her legs from all these voyages.

         And still it doesn't make her want
         to be laid up in port . . .

The poet in exile

129   . . . the Lesbians
            founded this great, conspicuous
            precinct for everybody, and
      set altars of the blest immortals there.

            They fixed the names of Suppliant Zeus,
            of thee, Aeolian goddess,* proud
            mother of all, and, for the third,
      of Dionysus who consumes raw flesh,

            Semele's son. Come now, all three,
            be well disposed and hearken to
            our prayer: deliver us from these
      discomforts that our cruel exile brings.

            Let Hyrrhas' son* be visited
            by our friends' vengeance, for we swore
            stern oaths that none of us would e'er
      betray a member of our company,

            but either lie in cloaks of earth,
            killed by those men who then held power,
            or else put them to death, and save
      the people from its burden of distress.

            But this Potbelly gave no thought
            to that. He's trampled on his oaths
            without a qualm, and ravages
      our city . . .

            not by the law that . . .
            pale-eyed A[thene(?) . . .
            writt[en . . .
      Myrsi[lus . . .

130b   Plunged in the wild chaste-woods I live
            a rustic life, unhappy me,
            longing to hear Assembly called
            and Council, Agesilaïdas!

            From lands my grandfather grew old
            possessing, and my father too,
            among these citizens who wrong
            each other, I've been driven away,

an outland exile: here I dwell
like Onomacles,* the Athenian
spear-wolf, out of the fray. To make
peace with . . . is not wise.

So to the precinct of the gods,
treading the dark earth . . .
. . . I live,
keeping well out of trouble's reach.

Now Lesbos' long-robed girls are here
for the beauty-contest. All around,
the women's wondrous annual cry,
the holy alleluia, rings.

When will the gods from all my trials
deliver . . .

360   It's like they say Aristodemus said
in Sparta once, a quite astute remark:
a man is what he owns; no pauper is
a man of quality or high esteem.

364   Poverty is a hard and unstoppable evil: she,
with her sister Resourcelessness, conquers a
     mighty host.

Schemes for action

306g   Now we must trust in fortune
and jump on Pittacus from behind.

206   But now Athena, daughter of great Zeus,

has given courage . . .
. . . set bowls for mixing wine
. . . have you bear that in mind
. . . has become apparent and . . .

. . . till Zeus and Destiny
. . . But fear

249   . . . firm-thwarted ship
. . . better not
. . . hold back the winds.

One should look out before one sails,
if one is able and has skill,
but once at sea, one's forced to ride what comes.

140   The high hall is agleam
with bronze; the roof is all arrayed
     with shining helms, and white
horse-plumes to ornament men's heads
     nod from their crests. Bright greaves
of bronze to keep strong arrows off
     cover the unseen pegs,
and corselets of new linen, and
     a pile of convex shields.
     Chalcidian swords are there,
and belts in plenty, tunics too.
     We can't forget this store
now that we've taken on this task.

383   Has Tyrrakos' son Dinnomenes
still got his gleaming kit in store
at Myrrhineum?

200   Zeus, Kronos' son, alone controls
the outcome of events.

361   And if Zeus fulfils our scheme . . .

314   The immortal gods . . .
victory to us.

391   Whoever are good men of you and us.

69   Vexed at our troubles, father Zeus!
     the Lydians pledged two thousand pounds
if we could get back to our holy town,

     though we had never helped them, and
     they knew us not. But that sly fox
who called it easy thought we would not guess . . .

Pittacus comes to power

332   Now we must drink with might and main,
get drunk, for Myrsilus is dead!

141   This fellow who seeks the high command will soon
turn the town upside down: it's poised to tilt.

74   While the log's
still only smoking, put the fire out.

351 But now this fellow's in charge, playing his final card.

348   Fitznobody Pittacus
they've made tyrant of that gutless and ill-starred town
with united acclaim.

70   But the lyre still plays
its sportive part at the symposium:
feasting with empty braggarts . . .

Well, he's now married into the Atreid line;*
let him destroy the city, like he did
with Myrsilus, till it's the War-god's will
that we take arms. Let's put rage out of mind,

and let's wind down this spirit-gnawing strife
of kith and kin that some Olympian's roused,
bringing the people to calamity
and Pittacus to enviable pomp.

Uncertain context

119 Who gave you cause, you wretch, to say
     . . . ?
     . . . Heaven's not to blame . . .
. . . falling short

in nothing: I restrained you from
your folly. So take heed of what
I say, and stop, and if you can,
keep . . . from the trouble that's at hand.

For your time now is past and gone,
and all your grapes are gathered in,
but it's a good plant, and there's hope
it will be bearing many a cluster yet—

when the time comes; for from a vine
like this . . .
     . . . I'm afraid
that they may pick the fruit before it's ripe.

Even so they who toiled before . . .

306A   . . . to us; you do no harm,
since you are gone, killed by the Alliens' blows.

And then you sacrificed (?) us, wretched boy.

As for Amardis, I am unconcerned,
     but more upset amid my drinking friends:
and for that bloodshed I am not at all
     to blame.

337 The first's Antandros the Lelegian town.

344 Yes, I certainly know I'm dislodging a rubble heap,
     not a stack of squared blocks; so he may get an
          aching head.

296a He deserves to be flayed more than Antileon.

298   . . . disgracing those
     who . . . wrong: we ought to set
his neck in clamps, and stone him . . .

     Much better for the Achaeans if
     they'd punished Aias' sacrilege*
     with death: when they were sailing home
past Aegae, they'd have had a gentler sea.

     For Priam's daughter* in the shrine
     of Plunderer Athena clasped
     the holy image, touched its chin
for safety, as the foes swept through the town.

     . . . and Deïphobus
     they'd slain; loud wailing could be heard
     from all the people on the walls,
and children's screams filled the Dardanian plain.

     Then Aias came, crazed fatally,
     into that shrine of Pallas, who
     of all the blessed gods is most
implacable to sacrilegious men.

     Seizing the maiden in his arms
     beside the sacred image where
     she stood, the Locrian dragged her forth,
not fearing Zeus's daughter, queen of war.

     But she frowned fierce beneath her brows,
     her face turned livid; out she went
     over the wine-dark sea, and there
began to stir up tempests unforeseen.

Songs about Troy

42   They tell that Priam and his sons
        found yours a bitter marriage-bond,
Helen, that sank fair Ilios in flames.

        How different was the graceful bride
        Aeacus' son* from Nereus' deeps
brought home to Chiron's cave, with all the gods

        guests at the wedding! He undid
        her virgin waistband: love grew well
for Peleus and the flower of Nereids.

        In time she bore a hero son
        to drive his tawny steeds in pride
while Troy and Trojans paid for Helen's sin.

44   . . . Pria[m's sons.]
        (Achilles) . . . called on his mother's name,*

        on the fairest of sea Nymphs, and in turn she at
             the knees of Zeus
        made entreaty, that he cure her dear son's anger
             and discontent.

283   and fluttered Argive Helen's heart
        within her breast. She, crazy for
the Trojan cheat-host, sailed away with him,

        abandoning her daughter dear
        and her rich husband's bed: the child
of Zeus and Leda heard the call of love.

        [Now Paris has his due.] The earth
        full many of his brothers keeps,
felled in the Trojan plain because of her.

        Many the chariots that hit
        the dust, many the bright-eyed lads
trampled, as prince Achilles gleed in blood.

387   Blood of the royal son of Kronos,
        Aias, who they say was the noblest
hero, after Achilles, [to fight at Troy].

388   and shaking a Carian helmet-plume

395   Corpse-choked the stream of Xanthus* reached the sea.

Drinking songs

38   Drink, be merry with me, Melanippus. What
          makes you think
      that, when once you have crossed over eddying
          Acheron,

      you will ever again get a glimpse of the sun's pure
          light?
      No, don't have big ideas . . .

      So once Sisyphus, Aeolus' son of the royal blood,
      that most canny of men, had a notion of cheating
          death,*

      but in spite of his cleverness fate for the second
          time
      sent him over the eddying waters of Acheron,

      and the lord of the earth, Kronos' son, for a
          punishment
      made him labour and toil. But enough of such
          ponderings.

      While we're young, above all, . . .
      . . . whatever of this must be borne . . .

      . . . north wind . . .

50   Slave-boy, trickle the scent over my long-suffering
          head for me,
      and my chest with its grey hairs . . .

      while we're drinking . . .

322   From Teian cups the wine-drops fly.

333   For wine's the window to see through a man.

334   and Poseidon has not yet
      convulsed the briny sea.

335   We must not brood upon our ills,
        Bycchis; repining will not help.
      The best cure's fetching wine and getting drunk.

338   Rain in the sky, foul weather coming down,
          the watercourses frozen . . .

> Defeat the weather: light a fire,
> mix the sweet wine unstintingly,
and put a nice soft cushion by my head.

342   Let the vine be the first fruit-tree you plant: others
         can wait their turn.

343   Water-nymphs, whom they say Zeus of the great
         aegis on high creates.

346   Let's drink! Why wait for the lamps? Only an inch
         of day.
Get those bigger cups down, boyo, the fancy ones.

Wine puts cares out of mind, gift of a god to men,
Zeus' and Semele's son. Water it two to one;

pour them full to the brim, cup after cup, without
any gap.

347   Wet your whistle with wine, boyo, the Dog-star's back;
it's a hard time of year, everything's parched with
         heat.

Pleasant out of the bush comes the cicada's noise,
and the thistle's in flower. Women are dirtiest

now, but men are reduced—Sirius dries the sap
from their head and their knees . . .

352   Let's drink! The Dog-star's round again.

358   If wine fetters the wits . . .
Often he hangs his head and blames himself,
regretting what he's said, but it's too late
to take it back.

359   Child of cliff and foaming sea

                .

O limpet, and you void lads of their wits.*

362   So someone hang around my neck
garlands of plaited dill, and pour
sweet myrrh down over my chest.

366   Wine, dear boy, and truth go hand in hand.

367   I've heard [the bird that announces] the coming of
         flowery spring,
so . . .

and mix a bowl of the honey-sweet, quick as ever
       you can.

368 Someone had better invite the delightful Menon
     if I'm to enjoy being in on the drinking party.

369 Sometimes it's honey-sweet when they draw it off,
     sometimes it's sharper than teasels.

374 Receive a reveller, I pray you, O receive me, I pray.

397 the bloom of (his?) tender fruit

401*a* Greetings: here's a cup to drink.

401*b* Come and drink with me.

Miscellaneous fragments

10 (*A woman sings*)
       Unhappy me, acquainted with all miseries,

                  .   .   .   .   .

       . . . a shameful death . . .
       For I am victim of a sore disablement;
       a frightened deer's cry forms itself
       within my breast, and raging . . .
       . . . perdition . . .

380 I fell by the arts of the Cyprian goddess.

115 . . . with birds from the lake to this town . . .
     from the . . . peaks, from where a fragrant . . .
     . . . cool water . . . vine-covered . . .
     . . . green reeds . . .
     . . . zephyr's bright spring sound . . .

117   What you give a whore,
     you might as well chuck in the foaming sea.

     Whoever knows this not can take my word:
     when you consort with whores, it turns out so,
     you have to make it up . . .
     with shame, accursed misery galore.

296*b* Opportunely the great goddess of love,
          Damoanaktidas,

breathed down gladness and joy on you by those
    beautiful olive-trees.
When spring opens its gates, . . . smell of ambrosia
                    . . . young men
                . . . hyacinth-garlanded.

317a   And you will have your [death?]
       in your own hands.

319   The untempestuous breath of feeble winds.

320   and naught would come of aught.

329   His helmet shot with gold,
       he nimbly d[ances]

336   Indeed, a blindstorm's snatched your wits away.

341   If you say what you like, maybe you'll hear
       answers you like much less.

345   What are these birds, come from the World
       Stream, from the ends of earth,
       these wild duck, dapple-necked, soaring on
         wide-stretched wings?

365   A great big stone, Aisimidas, is set
       over the head of Tantalus.

372   more martial than Ares.

375   Well, I can't find the witnesses to that.

376   And sitting by Dinnomenes
       you drain your cup.

377   You've made me forget my woes.

384   O flower-haired, pure, gently smiling sister.

393   Here's the pig provoking us again.

350 (*To his brother Antimenidas returning from Babylonian mercenary
service*)
    So you're back from the world's end, with an ivory
    sword-hilt fastened with gold . . .
    great achievement, and you rescued them from distress
    by dispatching a huge giant, just one palm off
    five imperial cubits!

354   Achilles, lord of the Scythian land.*

355   'twixt earth and snowy sky.

THEOGNIS

11–14   Artemis, huntress born of Zeus, whom
            Agamemnon
        founded here* as he set sail for Troy,
    hear thou my prayer, save me from harm: for thee
            it is
        a small thing, goddess, but so much to me.

19–26   When I make verses, Cyrnus, have them locked
            away—
        though if they're stolen, it will always show;
    no one will choose the bad where better is to
            hand,
        and all will say, 'This is Theognis' verse,
    from Megara': my name is famous everywhere—
        but some still criticize my statesmanship.
    No wonder, Polypaïdes: not even Zeus,
        whether he rains or no, can please them all.

27–30   I'm well disposed to you; I'll give you good advice
        that as a boy I learned from men of worth.
    Be sensible, and do not stoop to shameful deeds
        to seize yourself esteem, prestige, or wealth.

31–8   So that's that lesson. Next, do not consort with
            knaves,
        but hold fast always to the men of worth:
    drink among those, and eat, and sit with those,
            and seek
        their favour, who have wealth and influence.
    From sound men you will learn sound lessons: if
            you mix
        with rogues, you'll even lose what sense you
            have.
    Take this to heart, keep worthy company. Some
            day
        you'll grant I give my friends the best advice.

39–52   Cyrnus, this town's in labour—and I fear it may
      bring one to birth who'll right our wicked ways.
    The burghers here still keep their heads; their
      leaders, though,
      are heading for a catastrophic fall.
    No town was ever yet destroyed by men of worth,
      but when the rogues embrace unrighteousness,
    corrupt the people, and uphold dishonest claims
      for sake of private gain and influence,
    do not expect that city to stay quiet long,
      even if now it lies in utter calm,
    when things like that are chosen by dishonest
      men—
      gain that comes hand in hand with public ill.
    It leads to civil strife, bloodshed within the clan,
      dictators. May we never opt for that.

53–68 (+1109–14)
    Cyrnus, the town's a town still, but it has new
      folk
      who knew no justice previously, no laws.
    They used to wear old goatskins on their flanks,
      and lived
      outside the town like deer. And now they are
    the gentry, Polypaïdes, while yesterday's
      gentry are dregs. Who can support the sight—
    the men of worth reviled, the lower class esteemed?
      Good stock now seeks to marry into bad;
    men cheat each other, laughing at each other's
      loss,
      unable to distinguish good from ill.
    Make none of these your true friend, Polypaïdes,
      for any reason, these who live here now.
    Pretend in speech to be the friend of everyone,
      but share with no one anything at all
    that matters, or you'll find those wretched
      characters
      cannot be trusted in the reckoning.
    They have embraced deceit and lies and subtleties
      like men past all salvation, past all hope.

69–72   Never trust, Cyrnus, or consult a low-class man
         when you have some important goal in view.
         To find a good man you must be prepared to go
         a long way, Cyrnus, and to take great pains.

75–6   Trust few men, Cyrnus, in a weighty enterprise,
         or pain past curing may be your reward.

77–8   A trusty man is worth his weight in gold and silver,
         Cyrnus, when there's a crisis in the state.

79–82   You'll find few comrades, Polypaïdes, who prove
             dependable when things are difficult,
         men who can keep their nerve and bring
             themselves to share
         prosperity or hardship equally.

91–2   He's a bad comrade, Cyrnus, who, saying one
             thing, thinks
         another: better enemy than friend.

101–12   Let none persuade you, Cyrnus, to befriend a
             knave.
         What use is a rapscallion as a friend?
         He'll neither get you out of trouble and distress
         nor let you into any luck he has.
         Doing good turns to villains is love's labour lost:
         you might as well sow the grey sea with corn.
         You'll reap no heavy harvest if your field's the sea,
         and no reward from doing good to rogues.
         They're always wanting more; and if you once fall
             short,
         all thanks for previous favours drains away,
         whereas a man of worth appreciates a boon,
         remembers, and is grateful evermore.

117–18   A false man is the hardest thing to recognize,
         Cyrnus: there's nothing calls for greater care.

119–28   False gold or silver is a threat that can be checked,
         Cyrnus; an expert quickly finds it out;
         but if a comrade's secret disposition's false
         and in his breast he has an untrue heart,
         this is the basest counterfeit that God has put
         before us, and it costs most pain to test.

You cannot know a man's or woman's character
    until you've tried if it will bear a load,
nor can you judge as if inspecting merchandise:
    so often the appearances deceive.

129–30 Don't pray for status, Polypaïdes, or wealth:
    the only thing a man requires is luck.

131–2 One's parents are the greatest treasure in the world,
    Cyrnus, for all who value righteousness.

133–42 No one's responsible for his own gain or loss,
    Cyrnus: it is the gods that give us both,
and no man as he toils knows whether in the end
    his enterprise will turn out well or ill.
Often a man who thought he was to fail succeeds,
    while one who thought to be successful fails.
No man is handed everything that he desires;
    it cannot pass the limits of his means.
We mortals have no knowledge, only vain belief;
    the gods fix everything to suit themselves.

143–4 No man has ever cheated guest or suppliant,
    Cyrnus, without the immortals taking note.

145–8 Go for a righteous life without much property
    rather than wealth dishonestly acquired.
All honour, Cyrnus, is contained in honesty,
    and every honest man's a man of worth.

149–50 Even an utter villain, Cyrnus, may get wealth
    from Fortune, but true worth is shared by few.

151–2 Lawless behaviour, Cyrnus, is what God first gives
    to villains that he means to sweep away.

159–60 Cyrnus, don't ever talk too big, for no man knows
    what change another day and night may bring.

173–8 There's nothing gets a good man down like
        poverty,
    Cyrnus—not hoary age, nor fever chill.
Throw yourself, Cyrnus, to the monsters of the
        deep
    to escape it, or leap down the towering cliffs.
A man o'ercome by poverty is powerless
    in speech and action, and his tongue is tied.

179–80   Cross the earth, Cyrnus, cross the broad-backed
              sea likewise,
         to find release from painful poverty.

181–2   Better, dear Cyrnus, for a pauper to be dead
              than live oppressed by painful poverty.

183–92   With horses, rams, and asses, Cyrnus, we seek out
              good blood, and everyone wants pedigree
         to breed from; yet a man of class, if offered wealth,
              doesn't mind marrying from worthless stock,
         nor does a woman turn a base groom down, if he
              be rich: she chooses money over worth.
         Property's what they value. Good stock breeds from
              bad
              and bad from good; wealth has confounded
              blood.
         Don't be surprised then, Cyrnus, that the
              burghers' stock
              is fading: they're diluting good with bad.

219–20   Cyrnus, don't chafe too much because the town's
              astir,
         but walk the middle of the road, like me.

233–4   A man of worth's the witless people's citadel
              and rampart, Cyrnus, yet in slight esteem.

235–6   We're looking nothing like survivors any more,
              Cyrnus, but like a city doomed to fall.

237–54   For my part, I have made you wings on which to
              fly
         across the endless sea and all the earth
              with ease: you'll be at every dinner, every feast,
              and many a man will have you on his lips,
         and lovely lads accompanied by alto pipes
              will sing of you in voices sweet and clear
         and orderly. And when, down in the earth's dark
              nooks,
              you go to Hades' house of wailing grief,
         not even then in death will your fame fade, but
              men
              will always cherish your immortal name,

Cyrnus, as you roam over all the land of Greece
  and all the islands of the teeming sea,
not riding then on horseback; no, the
    violet-wreathed
  Muses will speed you by their noble grace.
Future men likewise, all who have an interest,
  will sing of you, while earth and sun exist.
And yet from you I cannot get some slight respect;
  you lie to me as if I were a child.

299-300 When ill befalls a man, none wants to be his
    friend,
  Cyrnus, though he be of the same womb born.

319-22 A good man, Cyrnus, has a firm and constant
    mind,
  and holds fast in good fortune and in ill,
but if God gives a base man livelihood and wealth,
  the fool can't stop his baseness coming out.

323-8 Never destroy a friendship on some trivial ground,
    Cyrnus, believing wicked slanderous tongues.
If one were angry with one's friends at every lapse,
  there'd be no friends, no mutual harmony;
for lapses are inherent in our mortal world,
  Cyrnus. Only the gods deny them space.

329-30 With planning, even a slow man overtakes the swift,
    Cyrnus, helped by the justice of the gods.

331-2 Be calm, like me, and walk the middle of the road,
    Cyrnus: give neither side the other's due.

333-4 Don't help an exile, Cyrnus, hoping for reward.
    Even back home he's not the man he was.

335-6 Don't fuss too much. The mid-position's always
    best,
  Cyrnus. You'll still have class: that's hard to
    steal.

337-40 Zeus grant I may repay my friends, who are so
    kind,
  Cyrnus, and even more my enemies.
I'd feel then like a god on earth, could I but get
  revenge before my appointed death-day comes.

355–60   Hold firm amid these setbacks, Cyrnus, as before
              when fortune sent you good things you rejoiced,
          and just as after good luck bad luck came, so seek
              to emerge once more by praying to the gods.
          Don't let it show too much. It's bad to let it show;
              you have few sympathizers for your plight.

361–2   A man's heart dwindles, Cyrnus, when disaster
              strikes,
              but when he gets revenge it grows again.

367–70 +1183–4
          There's no man, Cyrnus, that the sun's rays look
              upon
              who is not with some criticism tagged,
          but I can't understand the city's attitude:
              they're hostile whether I do right or wrong.
          Yes, plenty criticize me, both good men and base,
              but not one of the fools can match my style.

371–2   Don't ply the goad and force me, Cyrnus, to the
              yoke,
              pulling me too far into comradeship.

409–10   No greater treasure, Cyrnus, will you leave your
              sons
              than modesty, which clings to men of class.

411–12   Cyrnus, that friend is held inferior to none
              who is endowed with both good sense and
                  means.

429–38   It's easier to beget and rear a man than put
              good sense in him. No one has yet devised
          a way to make a fool wise, or a bad man good.
              If God had granted the Asclepiads*
          this power, to cure men's baseness and their
              blighted wits,
              they would be earning many a handsome fee.
          If man's mind could be crafted and put into place,
              no son of worthy sire would be a knave:
          he'd heed his words of wisdom. But one cannot
              teach
              a scoundrel to become respectable.

1101–2 +539–40

> Whoever counselled you about me and advised
>   forsaking my companionship, this man,
> dear Cyrnus, is but forging shackles for himself,
>   unless my judgement's clouded by the gods.

541–2

> Cyrnus, I fear that lawlessness may kill this town
>   as it did the brutish Centaurs long ago.

543–6

> I'll have to judge this case exactly by the rule,
>   Cyrnus, and give both sides their equal shares
> with help from seers and auguries and altar flames,
>   so that no error puts me in disgrace.

549–53

> The silent messenger* stirs woeful war to life,
>   Cyrnus, from yon high look-out blazing forth.
> So saddle up your steeds: I think they'll meet the
>   foe—
> it is not far—already on the road.

631–2

> The man whose head can't rule his heart is ever
>   found
>   in trouble, Cyrnus, and perplexity.

653–4

> May I have heaven's favour and the gods' good
>   will,
>   Cyrnus. I crave no status otherwise.

655–6

> At your misfortune, Cyrnus, all of us feel pain;
>   but troubles not one's own are soon forgot.

805–10

> An envoy sent to Delphi, Cyrnus, must take care
>   to be more true than scale or rule or lathe,
> that man to whom the priestess of the god imparts
>   the oracle from out the wealthy shrine.
> Any addition would negate the remedy,
>   and any cut would be a sacrilege.

811–14

> I've suffered something worse than—well, not
>   ugly death,
>   but bitterer, Cyrnus, than all other fates.
> My friends have let me down. So I must go and
>   try
>   my enemies, to see how they're disposed.

815–17

> An ox's mighty hoof upon my tongue prevents
>   my currying favour, though I know the art,

Cyrnus. And after all, what destiny ordains
that one must suffer, cannot be escaped.

819–20   Cyrnus, we've reached a crisis oft foreseen in
prayers.
Now may one death embrace the two of us.

821–2   There's little place for people who show disrespect
to parents, Cyrnus, when they're getting old.

833–6   It's all gone to the dogs, to ruin, and we can't
blame any of the immortal blessed gods,
Cyrnus. It's human violence, graft, and insolence
have cast us from success to misery.

895–6   Sense is the best thing that a man can have in him,
Cyrnus; insensibility the worst.

897–900   Cyrnus, if God were angry at each little thing
with mortals, knowing each man's private
thoughts
and all his actions, then it would go hard for us,
both righteous and unrighteous men alike.

1027–8   Disaster's easy to achieve in men's affairs,
Cyrnus, but hard the skill of making good.

1037–8   It is the hardest thing to cheat a man of worth,
Cyrnus. This view I came to long ago.

1103–4   Lawlessness broke Magnesia, Smyrna, Colophon,
Cyrnus: it's bound to break you people too.

1133–4   Cyrnus, while friends are by, let's check the ill at
start
and seek to cure the ulcer ere it grows.

1171–6   Sense, Cyrnus, is the gods' best gift to mortal men:
sense truly has the tabs on everything.
Lucky's the man who has it—far to be preferred
to accursed lawlessness or too much wealth.
That is a bane to mortals, there is nothing worse.
From such things, Cyrnus, comes all misery.

1177–8   Could you touch not base deeds and stay
untouched by them,
Cyrnus, you might best know the good man's
life.

1179–80   Cyrnus, respect the gods and fear them. This is
              what
          restrains a man from impious word and deed.

1197–1202
              O Polypaïdes, I hear the crane's shrill cry
                  telling men that it's time to plough and sow.
              It stabs my melancholy heart with pain, to think
                  my flower-bright farmland lies in other hands
              and I've no mules at work pulling the crooked
                  plough

1217–18   Perhaps one day he'll moan, and we'll sit by and
              grin,
          Cyrnus, rejoicing in our own success.

1219–20   Cyrnus, it's difficult to trick one's enemy,
              but easy for a friend to cheat a friend.

1221–2   Mortal men's calculation, Cyrnus, tends to make
              many a slip when judgement is disturbed.

1223–4   There's nothing, Cyrnus, more unjust than wrath:
              it gives
          the heart that shelters it ill recompense.

1225–6   There's nothing sweeter, Cyrnus, than a goodly
              wife.
          I can attest it: test it out yourself.

1353–5   Bitter and sweet is love, desirable and cruel
              to young men, Cyrnus, till it be fulfilled.
          If one succeeds, then it is sweet; but if pursuit
              finds no success, there is no sharper pain.

SOLON

Salamis*

1   I bring my own dispatch from lovely Salamis,
        adopting ordered verse instead of speech.

2   In that case I would rather be from Sikinos
        or Pholegandros,* no Athenian,
    for soon the word would go about, 'He's one of
        those
        Athenian Salamis-abandoners.'

3   Let's start for Salamis, fight for the lovely isle
        and free ourselves from terrible disgrace.

Other political poems

4   Our state will never fall by Zeus's ordinance
        or the immortal blessed gods' intent:
    such a stout-hearted guardian, she of the mighty
        sire,
        Pallas Athene, holds her hand above:
    but by their foolishness the citizens themselves
        seek to destroy its pride, from avarice,
    with the unprincipled mob-leaders, who are set
        to suffer badly for their great misdeeds.
    They know not how to prosper modestly, enjoy
        in festive peace the happiness they have.

       ·   ·   ·   ·   ·

    and they grow wealthy by unrighteousness.
    [When wicked men . . .]
        and, sparing neither sacred property
    nor public, seize by plunder, each one what he
        can,
        careless of Righteousness's august shrine—
    the silent one, who knows what is and has been
        done,
        and comes at last to claim the payment due—

this aims a sure blow at the whole community,
   and soon it comes to wretched slavery
which rouses war from sleep, and strife within the
      clan,
   and sunders many from their lovely youth.
For if men injure their own people, they soon find
   their lovely city scarred and faction-torn.
Among the populace these evils roam at large,
   and many of the poor folk find themselves
in foreign lands, sold into slavery and bound
   in shameful bonds . . .
And so the public ill comes home to every man:
   the yard doors are no more disposed to hold;
it leaps the high wall, and it finds him out for sure,
   though he take refuge in his inmost room.
This lesson I desire to teach the Athenians:
   Lawlessness brings the city countless ills,
while Lawfulness sets all in order as is due;
   many a criminal it puts in irons.
It makes the rough smooth, curbs excess, effaces
      wrong,
   and shrivels up the budding flowers of sin;
it straightens out distorted judgements, pacifies
   the violent, brings discord to an end,
brings to an end ill-tempered quarrelling. It makes
   all men's affairs correct and rational.

4*a*   I mark—and sorrow fills my heart upon the sight—
       the eldest country of Ionia*
      listing.

4*c*   And as for you, who now have all the wealth you
         want,
       make the stern spirit gentler in your hearts,
     adjust to moderation. We will not accept
       this state of things, nor will it work for you.

5   The commons I have granted privilege enough,
       not lessening their estate nor giving more;
    the influential, who were envied for their wealth,
       I have saved them from all mistreatment too.

I took my stand with strong shield covering both
     sides,
   allowing neither unjust dominance.

6   Thus would the commons and its leaders best
       accord,
     not given too free a rein, nor pushed too hard.
   Surplus breeds arrogance, when too much wealth
       attends
     such men as have no soundness of intent.

7   Hard to please everyone in politics.

9   As from the cloudbank comes the storm of snow or
       hail,
     and thunder follows from the lightning flash,
   exalted men portend the city's death: the folk
     in innocence fall slave to tyranny.
   Raise them too high, and it's not easy afterwards
     to hold them. Now's the time to read the signs.

10 A short time now will show the Athenians how
       mad
     I am,* when truth comes out for all to see.

11 If by your own fault you have suffered grief and
       harm,
     put no part of the blame upon the gods.
   You raised these men up,* by providing
       bodyguards,
     and that's why wretched slavery's your lot.
   Your trouble is, each of you treads the fox's way,
     but your collective wits are thin as air.
   You watch a crafty fellow's tongue, and what he
       says,
     but fail to look at anything he does.

12 It's by the winds the sea's disturbed: if nobody
     stirs it, it stays of all things best-behaved.

13 Bright daughters of Olympian Zeus and Memory,
     Pierian Muses, hearken to my prayer.
   Grant me that I have fortune from the blessed
       gods,
     and good repute from all men all the time;

may I be honey to my friends, gall to my foes,
   honoured on sight or feared respectively.
Wealth I desire, but not to hold unrighteously,
   for surely sometime retribution comes.
The riches that the gods give are dependable
   from top to bottom of the storage jar,
but those that mortals cultivate with violence
   come awkward and unwilling at the call
of crime, and soon are tangled in calamity,
   which from a small beginning grows like fire,
a trifling thing at first, but grievous in the end,
   for mortal violence does not live long.
Zeus supervises every outcome. Suddenly
   like a March wind he sweeps the clouds away,
a gale that stirs the billowing ocean to its bed
   and ravages the tidy fields of wheat
before ascending to the gods' high seat in heaven,
   and then, behold, the sky is clear again:
the strong sun shines out on the fertile countryside
   in beauty; not a cloud remains to see.
Such is the punishment of Zeus. He does not flare
   at every insult, like a mortal man,
but all the time he is aware whose heart is marked
   with sin, and in the end it shows for sure.
One pays at once, another later; and if some
   escape the gods' pursuing fate themselves,
it comes sometime for sure: the innocent will pay—
   their children, or their later family.
Whether of high or low degree, we mortals think
   our various vanities are running well
until some blow falls; then we moan. But up to then
   we take fond pleasure in our empty hopes.
Whoever is oppressed by comfortless disease
   gets the idea he will return to health.
A man of low esteem imagines it is high;
   an ill-shaped man is proud of his good looks;
propertyless, and in the grip of poverty,
   he still has fancies of acquiring wealth.
They bustle on their different ways: one roams the
     sea

hoping to bring some profit home from trade,
tossed by tempestuous winds where fishes wait
    below,
  with no concession made to life and limb.
Another carves the soil—his business is the
    plough—
  and slaves away till fruit-time ends the year;
another's learnt Athena's and Hephaestus' craft,*
  and earns a living by his handiwork.
Another has been taught the Olympian Muses'
    boon,
  skilled in the rules of lovely poesy;
another one the lord Apollo's made a seer,
  who sees disaster coming from afar,
if he is favoured by the gods; but what is doomed
  no augury or sacrifice averts.
Others are healers, Paeon's office, well resourced
  in drugs: they too can give no guarantees.
Often a minor pain becomes an agony
  that cannot be relieved by soothing drugs,
whereas another, crazed by terrible disease,
  under the doctor's hands is quickly cured.
Fate brings to mortal men both good and ill: the
    gifts
  the immortals give are inescapable.
There's risk in every undertaking. No one knows,
  when something starts, how it will finish up.
One man makes noble efforts, but despite them
    all
  falls into unforeseen calamity;
another handles ill, yet God gives him complete
  success, freed from his folly's consequence.
But as to wealth, no limit's laid down clear for
    men,
  since those among us who possess the most
strive to earn double. Who could satisfy them all?
  Remember, profit's in the immortals' gift,
but loss's source is in men's selves: when sent by
    Zeus
  to punish them, it comes to each in turn.

14   Nor yet is any mortal fortunate, but all
         are wretched that the sun looks down upon.

15   For many curs are rich, and men of class are poor,
         but we'll not take their riches in exchange
      for our nobility, which always stays secure,
         while wealth belongs to different men by turns.

16   But wisdom's hidden formula, which holds the key
         to all things, is the hardest to discern.

17   The gods' intent is hidden every way from man.

18   As I grow old I'm always learning more.

19 (*To Philocyprus, king of Soloi in Cyprus*)
      But now I wish you many years of life and rule
         in Soloi here, you and your family:
      to me may Cypris* of the violet garland grant
         a safe, swift voyage from this famous isle.
      Favour and glory on this settlement may she
         bestow, and fair return to my own land.

20*   'I pray my death may catch me at threescore
         years'?
      If you'll still listen to me, take that out—
         don't mind me having wiser thoughts than
         you—
      and change it, Ligyastades, and sing,
         'I pray my death may come at fourscore years.'

21   Nor may my death come unlamented: when I die,
         I want to leave my friends with grief and groans.

22*a* And please tell tawny-haired young Critias* to
         heed
      his father—he'll be taking no bad guide.

23   Happy the man who has his sons, his hounds,
         his horses, and a friend from foreign parts.

24   Equally rich is he who has abundancy
         of silver, gold, and acres under plough,
      horses and mules, and he that only has the means
         to eat well, couch well, and go softly shod,
      and by and by enjoy a lad's or woman's bloom,
         with youth and strength still his to suit his need.

This is a man's true wealth: he cannot take all those
    possessions with him when he goes below.
No price he pays can buy escape from death, or
        grim
    diseases, or the onset of old age.

25   While youth's delight still flowers, and one loves a
        lad,
    sweet lips and thighs the object of desire.

26   But now I like the gods of love and wine and song
    and what they do for human happiness.

27   A boy, an ungrown child, in seven years puts forth
    a line of teeth and loses them again;
but when another seven God has made complete,
    the first signs of maturity appear.
In the third hebdomad he's growing yet, his chin
    is fuzzy, and his skin is changing hue,
while in the fourth one, each achieves his peak of
        strength,
    the thing that settles whether men are men.
The fifth is time a man should think of being wed
    and look for sons to carry on his line;
and by the sixth he's altogether sensible,
    no more disposed to acts of fecklessness.
With seven hebdomads and eight—fourteen more
        years—
    wisdom and eloquence are at their peak,
while in the ninth, though he's still capable, his
        tongue
    and expertise have lost some of their force.
Should he complete the tenth and reach the
        measured line,
    not before time he'd have his due of death.

28   There I dwelt
at the Nile's mouth, hard by Canopus' shore.

29   Poets say much that's false.

30   Rulers must be obeyed, however right or wrong.

31   First let us pray to Zeus, to Kronos' son the king,
    to grant these laws success and high prestige.

32 (*To Phocus*)
                              If I have spared
    my country, if I've not disgraced my name
    by grasping brute force and dictatorship,
    I'm not ashamed: this way I think I'll win
    more people over.

33   I know many people say
    'Solon is a stupid fellow, not a man who thinks
        ahead:
    God has offered him a fortune, but he hasn't taken
        it.
    There he had the prey encircled, but he didn't
        close the net—
    lost his nerve, no doubt about it, and his common
        sense as well.
    I'd not mind, if I'd seized power and the city's
        lavish wealth
    and become the lord of Athens even for a single
        day,
    being flayed to make a wineskin, with my family
        wiped out.'

34 Others came along for plunder. They had hopes of
        being rich,
    every one of them expecting he would make his
        fortune there
    and that I, for all my cooing, would reveal a harsh
        intent.
    After those vain calculations now they're furious
        with me,
    and they all look sideways at me, just as if I were
        their foe—
    wrongly. The decrees I uttered had the blessing of
        the gods,
    and I took no foolish further measures, since I
        have no taste
    by dictator's force to . . . or to see our fruitful
        land
    portioned out to good-for-nothings equally with
        men of worth.

36   Those aims for which I called the public meeting—
which of them, when I stopped, was still to
      achieve?
I call as witness in the court of Time
the mighty mother of the Olympian gods,
dark Earth, from whom I lifted boundary-stones*
that did beset her—slave before, now free.
And many to Athena's holy land
I brought back, sold abroad illegally
or legally, and others whom their debts
had forced to leave, their speech no longer Attic,
so great their wanderings; and others here
in ugly serfdom at their masters' mercy
I set free. These things I did in power,
blending strength with justice, carried out
all that I promised. I wrote laws for all,
for high and low alike, made straight and just.
But if another man had got the goad,
someone imprudent or acquisitive,
he'd not have checked the mob. If I'd agreed
to what the opposition favoured then,
and then to what the other party thought,
this city would be mourning many dead.
Therefore I turned to guard my every side,
a wolf at bay amid a pack of hounds.

37   If I must spell out where the mob's at fault,
they never would have dreamt what they have
      now

    .   .   .   .   .

while all the bigger and the stronger men
would then approve of me and call me friend.
For if another man had got the goad,
he'd not have checked the mob, or been content
until he'd churned the milk and lost the cream.
I marked the frontier in the No Man's Land
between these warring parties.

38   . . . they drink; and some of them eat cakes,
some bread, and others pastries mixed with lentils.
Nor are they lacking any sort of bake

that the dark earth provides for mortal men,
but everything is freely there at hand.

39–40   Some run for the mortar,
others for pickles, or for vinegar,
or pomegranate-seeds, or sesame.

ATTRIBUTED TO HOMER:
MARGITES

1   There came to Colophon a wonderful old bard,
     page of the Muses and Apollo, Archer-god,
        with a melodious lyre in his hands.

2 (*About Margites*)
     The gods had never taught him how to plant or
        sow
     or any other skill: he failed at every craft.

3   He knew a lot of things, but never knew them
        right.

5*   The fox knows lots of tricks,
     the hedgehog only one—but it's a winner.

7   . . . bladder (?). Hand outstretched,
     [he took his dick and set it to] the pot, and thrust
     [it in. Now in two] pinches he was caught:
     [his hand was stuck,] he could not get it out,
     [and he was bursting.] Well, he soon pissed in the
        pot
     . . . he had a new idea:
     . . . flung the doors open, and rushed out
     . . . through the dark of night
     [seeking to free his dick] and free his hand.
     . . . through the dark of night
     . . . [he r]an without a torch
     . . . unlucky he[ad]
     . . . thought it was a stone
     . . . and with forceful hand
     . . . [sma]shed the pot [thereon.]

ARISTOXENUS

And which sort of men are the biggest of pseuds
and the biggest of charlatans? Seers!

Sixth Century

STESICHORUS

The Funeral Games for Pelias

178   Hermes gave Castor the steeds
    Phlogeos and Harpagus, the swift foals of Podarga,
    and Hera gave Xanthus and Cyllarus.

179a *(Gifts for a girl)*
    sesame-cakes and spelt, sweetflan and other bakes
    and yellow honey.

179b   Amphiaraus won the long jump,
    Meleager the javelin.

The Song of Geryon*

S 14   [None of the gods] remained by Zeus
    the lord of all.

    Then did pale-eyed Athena
    speak to her stern-hearted uncle
    Poseidon, god of horse-ways:
    'Remember the promise you made,
    [and do not seek to save] Geryones from death.'

184 (S 7)
    . . . his cowherd Eurytion, born of . . .
    on the mainland, across from famed Erythea,
    by the boundless silver-veined waters of Tarshish
        river*
    in a cave in the rock.

S 8   Over the waves of the salty deep they came
    to the beautiful Isle of the Gods,
    where the Hesperides have their golden houses.

S 13 (*Geryones' parents appeal to him not to fight Heracles*)

> '. . . my unhappy motherhood, unhappy fate.
> Now I beg you, Geryones,
> if ever I gave you my nipple

> .   .   .   .   .   '

> [She drew apart her fragr]ant robe . . .

S 11   [With these words he] reached out . . .
> He spoke in answ[er, the powerful son]
> [of im]mortal [Chrysaor and Callirhoe:]

> 'Do not try to frighten me
> [by speaking of icy de]ath,
> and do not . . .
> Perhaps my [lineage makes me immortal, un]aging,
> [fit to live] in Olympus:
> if so, better [to fight and avoid] reproach

> [than to look on while the cattle]
> [are pl]undered from my [stalls.]
> Or if, dea[r father, all that's left]
> [for me is] carrying on into old age
> as one of those who live fr[om day to day,]
> [cut off fr]om the blessed gods,
> then now's the finest time to face my destiny

> [and save you] and all our kin
> from disgrace with men of the future [who tell]
> of the son of Chrysaor—
> may that not be the choice of the blessed gods.
> . . . fight for my cattle . . .'

S 15   . . . debated in his mind
> . . . to be best by far
> to . . . and fight by stealth

> against an enemy of such great might.
> . . . he planned
> a bitter end for him.
> . . . held his shield before
> . . . and from his head
> . . . the horsehair plume
> . . . upon the ground.

(13 lines lost)

(Heracles' arrow) bearing on its head
a charge of horrid death,
being besmeared with blood and . . . gall,
the torments of the deadly Hydra's darting heads.
In silent stealth he drove it in his brow,
cleaving the flesh and bones
by fortune's dispensation.
Straight through to his skull-top the shaft kept
    course,
and spoiled with crimson blood
his cuirass and his gory limbs.

Geryones bent his neck aslant
even as a poppy whose delicate structure
decays, and its petals soon fall.

185 (S 17)

    As the mighty Sun-god stepped into his bowl
of gold, to cross the river of World's End
to the holy deeps of Night
to his mother, his wedded wife, his dear children,
the son of Zeus took his way*
into the laurel-shaded grove.

181 (S 19)

    Then Heracles took the goblet, a three-flagon
        measure,
that Pholos* had mixed and served him,
and drank with application.

Helen

187   They showered quinces on the king's wedding car,
        they showered myrtle leaves,
        rose-garlands, crinkled wreaths of violet.

188   A silverstone foot-basin.

Palinodes*

193(a)   Hither once more, song-loving goddess.

193(b)   Gold-wingèd virgin Muse . . .

192   This tale they tell's not true:
        you did not sail in those benched ships
        or come to the towers of Troy.

Eriphyle*

S 148   The warrior Adrastus
         addressed him chidingly:
         'Alcmaeon, whither away, leaving the banqueters
         and this most excellent minstrel? Why
         have you risen from your place?'

         So he spoke, and the War-god's favourite,
         Amphiaraus' son, replied:
         'You stay, friend, drink, and keep your heart
         cheerful in feasting; but I've a task
                                                    ´

         and . . . how his mother
         harnessed a mule-cart and set off to Sicyon
         to seek a bride for him,

         . . . Anaxandros' daughter, of the line
         of haughty . . .

The Sack of Troy

S 88   'To the temple, the citadel, hasten,
        you Trojans and allied contingents,
        come, let us not be persuaded to . . .
        . . . uncouthly disfigure this . . . horse,
        the goddess's holy adornment:
        let us beware the Lady's heavy wrath,
                  .   .   .   .   .   ´

        So he spoke, and the Trojans . . .
        considered how . . .
        the great horse . . .

S 89   'But now by the waters of [fair-flowing] Simoïs
        we have been sorely befooled by a man
        who by the grace of the goddess, august Athena,
        knows the measures and skill . . .
        [Trickery] instead of battle
        and combat [will have] the great glory of
                 bringing
        on Troy of the broad dancing-places
        its day of captivity.'

S 105   . . . the Danaans eagerly sprang from the horse
         . . . Poseidon the holy earth-rider [sent
                 tremors (?);]
         Apollo [abided no longer in] holy [Ilios,]
         nor Artemis, nor Aphrodite
         . . . the Trojans' city Zeus . . .
         . . . Trojans . . .

Returns of the Heroes

209*   The lady Helen
         [cried out] at the sudden sight of the heavenly
                 sign,
         and these were her words to Odysseus' son:
         'Telemachus, this is surely some messenger from
                 on high,
         flown down through the fathomless air and gone
         screeching away with the voice of killing death.
         Even thus will Odysseus appear in your house
         . . . by the will of Athena.

         [But if you thin]k "this is but a chattering crow",
         [set off for ho]me, I will not hold you here.
         Penelope [will rejoice] to see you,
         son of the man she loves.'

The Orestes saga

210   Join me, Muse, in rejecting stories of battle,
         and celebrate weddings of gods and banquets of
                 men
         and feasts of the blessed.

211   when the swallow in springtime rings out.

212   Such are the lovely-haired Graces' gifts to the
                 public
         that we must sing, devising an elegant Phrygian
                 melody,
         at the arrival of spring.

217 (Apollo to Orestes)
         'I will give you this bow,*
         informed by all my arts,
         for victory in shooting.'

219*   She dreamed a serpent came, with a bloody wound
       on the crown of its head; and out of that
       appeared a king of Pleisthenes' line.

The Hunters of the Boar*

221   and buried its snout's tip beneath the ground.

222   . . . the sons of Thestios.

        [Five of] the youngest, their parents' darlings,
        [remain]ed at home, but the brave,
        fleet-footed Procaon and Clytius went.
        From Larisa came Eurytion,
        the son of long-robed . . .

        and the fierce son of Elatus

                        .   .   .

        On one side sat the Locrian spearsmen
        . . . the dear sons of . . .
        trusty Achaeans . . . and proud . . .
        and those who dwelt in Boeotia's holy acres;

        while on the other side the Dryopes
        and steadfast Aetolians . . .

The Sons of Oedipus*

222b (Jocasta speaking)

                'Do not add to my woes the burden of worry,
                or raise grim prospects for my future life.

                For the immortal gods
                have not ordained for men on this holy earth
                unchanging enmity for all their days,
                no more than changeless love;
                they set men's outlook for the day.
                As to your prophecies, I pray the lord Apollo
                will not fulfil them all;

                but if I am destined to see
                my sons slain by each other, if the Fates
                have so dispensed, then may
                death's ghastly close be mine straightway
                before I can ever behold
                the terrible moaning and tears of such woes,

my sons killed in the house
or the city fallen.

But come, dear sons, and hearken to my words.
Here's how I declare the outcome for you:
one to have the palace and live
by [the streams of Dirce], the other
to go hence, taking all your dear father's gold
and property—whichever of you two
draws the first lot by Destiny's design.

This, I think, should prove
the way to free you from an evil fate
as this godly seer foretells,
if truly Kronos' son [is to preserve]
King Cadmus' people and city, and put off
to later times whatever ill
is fated for our clan.'
So spoke the lady with appeasing words,
seeking to check her sons from combat in the
        house,
and the seer Teiresias supported her.
They agreed to do . . .

                (38 lines fragmentary)

. . . cattle and horses
. . . portion.

. . . what is destined to happen.
[Make your way to the hous]e of King Adrastus;
he will receive you, and give his lovely daughter
. . . and his people will give . . .'

                (12 lines fragmentary)

So spoke the famous [Teiresias], and at once
        the hero
departed from the house.
[The finest captains] of Thebes [escorted]
Polynices their friend.

He went upon his way, passed through the mighty
        wall
. . . with him . . .

            .   .   .   .   .

[By the gods'] guidance they reached the Isthmus,
the sea-[god's . . . with pr]ayers;

Then [they passed] Corinth's fair settlements,
and soon they came to [well-built] Cleonae.

From unidentified poems

223   because Tyndareos once,
when making sacrifice to all the gods,
forgot but one—the Cyprian who bestows
such amiable blessings. She in wrath
made his daughters twice- and thrice-marriers,
deserters of their men.*

232   Truly, above all
Apollo loves amusement, song and dance;
grief and lament are Hades' affair.

233   Shining in armour the new-born Pallas sprang
on to the broad earth.

235   Poseidon, the commander
of hollow-hoof horses.

240   Come, hither, Calliope pure of voice.

243   And the slim javelins
they hurled also.

244   For it is fruitless, it is helplessness,
to weep for the dead.

245   When a man is dead,
all favour he enjoyed is gone for nought.

250   O Muse who startest the dance . . .

P. Oxy. 3876 fr. 4
. . . and addressed her:
'Noble daughter of [Thestios,]*
it is no enviable news
you are about to receive in your halls.
This day your brothers are untimely dead,
slain by [your own dear son,]
the doughty [Meleager.']

Ibid. fr. 61–2

> [They] ba[thed his body well]
> [in warm water, and anointed it]
> with unguent of nectar fragrance . . .
> About him the cousin of Aeolus-Hippotades
> wrapped a long robe, and laid him out on clean
> fabrics. Then he concerned himself to build
> a pyre for the dead man: long branches he
>   gathered,
> and kindling . . .

Ibid. fr. 64b

> . . . battle . . .
> For a city is greatly en[hanced]
> when God bestows blessings upon it:
> there's no prestige or attainment for mortals
> beyond the divine allocation. A very clear sign
> . . . and of fighting . . .

282 . . . the famous and prosperous city
of Dardanid Priam they ravaged,
coming from Argos
by mighty Zeus' decision

in conflict well known to the poets
as woeful battle they waged
for Helen's auburn beauty,
and Ruin climbed up to long-suffering Pergamos
thanks to the Love-goddess golden-haired.

But I'm not concerned now with singing of Paris
the cheat-host, nor yet of Cassandra
slender of ankle
and Priam's other children,

or high-gated Troy's day of capture, ill-omened,
nor yet will I take as my subject
heroes of valour
and pride, whom ships full-bellied,

much-riveted, brought for the downfall
of Troy, those warriors brave
whom mighty Agamemnon
commanded, the Pleisthenid leader and
    sovereign,
excellent son sprung of Atreus' stock.

Those topics the skilled Heliconian Muses
could easily cover in story,
but a mere mortal
could never tell the details

of all of the ships that set sail out of Aulis
across the Aegean from Argos
out to the horse-plains
of Troy, and sailing in them

the bronze-shielded sons of Achaea.
The best of them with the spear

was fleet-of-foot Achilles
and great Telamonian Ajax the powerful
. . . fire.

But as to the handsomest man of the Argives
who travelled to Troy, [Cyani]ppus

> . . . .
> . . . .

[and also Zeuxippus, whom] Hyllis gold-girdled
gave birth to; his eye-catching beauty
Trojans and Danaans
compared with Troilus's,

like thrice-refined orichalc pitted
against the splendour of gold.
Their beauty is for ever;
and you too shall have fame undying,
    Polycrates,*
if we trust song and my own repute.

S 166   . . . they sang to the pipes
. . . luxury
. . . [year]ning as of love.

. . . .

The powers above bestow [lasting] prosperity
on whom they choose; for others [the reverse]
by Destiny's design.

[Quickly] the chieftains assembled with
the Tyndarids, when to the trumpet's command
for [Castor] breaker of horses and p[ugilist Pollux]
their godlike [followers rallied,]
and the great gold-aegis [Athena escorted them all]
on their way to woe[ful war.]

But that cannot be told [except]
by children of [the immortals]; whereas you
. . . fairest of men on earth
the sun looks down upon, godlike in form.
No other is so . . .
either among Ionians or . . .

. . . dwell in Lacedaemon,
land of fine men . . .

. . . with dancing and horses . . .
Here one can gaze on the deep
Eurotas, and round about, a marvel of beauty,
. . . leafy groves of f[irs]
. . . gardens

where they wrestle and run . . .
. . . train[ed] for the foot-race . . .

S 220   sweet pretension of love . . .
as if to one toiling in the race . . .

S 221   May this toil ever be mine.
And if someone finds fault with me
behind my back, I boast of that still more
. . . dark grudging . . .

S 222   [? smite me with a] club . . .
Not even were he cloaked
in the darkling woes of Oedipus or Ino
would he be deprived of his passion.

S 223(a)   [flew] up from the earth to [the pea]k,
cleaving the airy deep.

S 224 (Troilus)
that lad like to the gods,
whom he slew outside the towers of Ilios.

S 257(a) fr. 1
. . . songs praising you. Amid
delightful rosebuds, Charm, you raised him
by the shrine of Aphrodite;
fragrant the [flowers,] I must deem,
from which attentively she did anoint the boy,
and tender beauty was his gift
from those two goddesses.

But Equity [stayed out of that festivity:]
therefore I am weighed down,
and pass my sleepless nights
with mind astir.

S 257 (a) fr. 27

> The pipe . . .
> An ornate so[ng distils]
> from the Pierian Muses [into my mind;]
> and in it I'll sing of a lad . . .
> eyes . . . downy . . .
> when early Dawn of the white . . .
> [goes] up into [heaven to bring]
> [light for mortals] and gods . . .

S 257 (a) fr. 29+31

> Eros . . . the girl . . .
> unless he went down to her chamber one day
> and was thoroughly tinged in his melting heart
> with his expert mother's sweet gift of desire.
> Happy is he who can bring her the favour
> . . . whether her sister's child . . .

283   And he sat for a long time, paralysed
      by amazement.

285   Again, I killed the white-horsed
      sons of Moliona,*
      alike in age and features, one in body,
      both born together in a white-skinned egg.

286   In spring the Cydonian quince-trees
      watered from freshets of rivers
      where Nymphs have their virginal gardens
      blossom, and vine-shoots are growing
      under the shade of the branches;
      but Love in me at no season is laid to rest.

      Like the North Wind of Thrace that comes blazing
      with lightning, he rushes upon me,
      sent by the Cyprian goddess
      with withering frenzies, dark-lowering,
      undaunted, and from the foundations
      he overwhelms and devastates my heart.

287   Once again Love, as he looks at me meltingly
      under dark eyelashes, tries to induce me
      with every enticement to enter the Cyprian
      goddess's endless hunting-net.

By heaven, I tremble upon his approach
like a champion horse who is feeling his age
and is led once again to the chariot-yoke for a race.

288   Euryalus, scion of blue-eyed Graces,
darling of lovely-haired spirits of ripeness,
the Cyprian goddess and soft-eyed Temptation
raised you in beds of roses.

289b   And he soars in the unfamiliar void.

298   Heracles, Zeus' defender
with the supreme father's daughter, doughty Pallas;
for Zeus himself gave birth to her—
she sprang from the crown of his head.

302   He lay with Cadmus' daughter.

303a   [As long as] mortals talk
of the blue-eyed Cassandra, Priam's
daughter with lovely tresses.

303(b)   When the wakeful sonorous morning twilight
rouses the nightingales.

310   I fear I may do some wrong by the gods
in accepting such honour from men.

311   [if someone] with Strife's uncontrollable mouth
should arm for battle against me.

312   to swallow thick eddies of rain.

313   Once men have passed away,
then there's no cure to be found to bring back life.

314   Ablaze, like the sparkling stars through the hours
of night.

315   Myrtle, violet, helichryse,
apples, roses, and gentle bay.

316   They . . . undoing their gay embroidered
dresses, their veils and pins.

317(a)   On its topmost leaves sit ornate, dapple-throated
wild duck and purpleflash, long-winged
kingfishers.

317(b)   . . . me always, my heart,
as when the long-winged purpleflash . . .

319   scion of the War-god.

320   Nor Cyaras, the Medes' commander.

321   Along land built of stone
           collected by human hands,
           where formerly ravening fish
           kept company with sea-snails.

330   If it keeps clear of the wave-tops,
           no rope comes to harm.

335   War-dancers steadfast in the clash of arms.

336   The slender pillars of the sky.

339   The Laconian girls, who show their thighs.

ANACREON

346 fr. 1(*a*)

> but your heart's a-flutter on
> another, O boy of the beautiful face.

> And your [mother] fancies she
> has you closeted [at home,]
> whereas you [are secretly roaming abroad]

> in the fields of hyacinth,
> where the Cyprian from her yoke
> has fastened her . . . steeds.

> But you smashed [your chariot]
> in the middle [of the race—]
> [the car] that has half of the town in suspense.

346 fr. 1(*b*)

> Herotima, you public, public road.

346 fr. 4

> And I was sparring with a hard
> [partner; but now] I look up and lift my head.
> [To . . .] I owe much gratitude
> . . . having escaped from Love
> . . . altogether, and . . .
> . . . harsh bonds due to Aphrodite.
> . . . must bring wine . . . jar(s)
> . . . and bring water that splashes . . .

347

> . . . and the hair that
> shaded your delightful neck.*

> Now you're sneaped: that hair has fallen
> into scurvy hands, cascaded
> all at once into the dirt,

> ill-met with the blade of iron,
> and I'm heartsick: what's to do, if
> even pleas for Thrace don't work?

> As I hear, that famous lady
> is distraught, and keeps repeating,
> as she rails against her lot,

'How I wish you'd take me, mother,
to the cruel sea, and drop me
in the surging purple waves.'

348   Shooter of deer, I supplicate you,
Artemis, Zeus's fair-haired daughter,
mistress of beasts of the wild.

Now by the waters of Lethaeus*
you must be looking down with pleasure
on a city of men bold-hearted:
they are no wild and untamed people
that you have for your flock.

349   Here he is carping again
at the men of Ialysus with their sable shields.

351   They wantonly harass the doorman.

352   The amiable Megistes ten months now
wears osier wreaths and drinks the honeysweet must.

353   Confabulators across the island, Megistes,
are running the holy city.

354   And you will make me
the talk of the neighbours.

355   Tantalus' talents
he weighs in his balance.

356(a) Come, boy, bring us a bowl
so I can drink a sconce.
Pour in ten ladlesful
of water, five of wine,
so I can bacchanize
once more with no disgrace.

356(b) Come now, this time let's drink
not in this Scythian style
with din and uproar, but sip
to the sound of decent songs.

357   Lord, with whom the frisky Eros
sports, and the dark-eyed Nymphs, and the pink-
glowing goddess of love,

as you roam across the mountains' lofty
summits, I make supplication

to you, to come with kindly favour
to hear my gracious prayer:

stand by Cleobulus, and be his
wise adviser, O Dionysus:
make him accept my love.

358   Once again the gold-haired Eros
targets me with his crimson playball
and invites me to sport with a certain
     braided-sandalled girl.

But she, being from the noble island
of Lesbos, only turns her nose up
at my white hair; she is gawping
     after some other lass.

359   Cleobulus is who I love,
Cleobulus I'm mad about,
Cleobulus I ogle.

360   O lad with the look of a lass,
I seek you, but you don't heed,
not knowing you hold the reins
     of my soul, my life.

361   Myself, I wouldn't want to have
          the Horn of Plenty, or to be
king of Tarshish for a hundred and fifty years.

362   We're into the midwinter month;
the cloud's heavy with rain, the rough storms
     rumble.

363   Why then do you fly
with your chest that's hollower than a pipe
anointed with sweet myrrh?

368   You wheel towards Leucippe.

364   For Thargelius says
you throw a neat discus.

366   But O my Smerdies, that have
got yourself scrubbed out over and again.

367   For you were obdurate regarding me.

370   Neither my tender sister . . .

371   Nor am I even-tempered
      or nice to my fellow men.

372   And auburn Eurypyle's interested in
      that litter-borne Artemon.

373   For breakfast I broke off a bit of sweet sesame cake;
      I've drunk a whole flagon of wine, and in luxury
            now
      I play my sweet harp, making merry beside my
            dear girl.

374   I pluck my twenty-stringed harp, striking an octave
            chord;
      and you just are, young Leucaspis.

375   Who can turn his mind to the loveliness
      of youth, and dance to the slender half-hole pipes?

376   Once more I leap up from the White Cliff,
      drunk with love, and plunge in the foaming
            waves.

377   And the Mysians
      discovered mare-mounting by asses.

378   Well, I'm flying up to heaven on airy wings
      due to love, because . . . won't share his youth
            with me.

379   Love, seeing me with greying beard, flies past;
      I feel the draught of his gold-gleaming wings.

380   All hail, dear light, smiling with lovely face.

381   Dropping my shield by a fair river's banks.

382   And took to heart the tearful spear.

383   The slave-girl served honeysweet wine
      into a three-measure goblet.

384   Nor had Persuasion begun at that time
      to shine with a silvery light.

385 (*A woman sings*)
      I'm just coming back from the river
      with all my washing clean.

386   I noticed Sīmalus in the dance
      holding a pretty harp.

387   I asked the perfumer Strattis if he
      was going to grow any hair.

388   He used to wear a rough cloak, pinched in at the
           waist,
      and wooden baubles in his ears, and round his ribs
       a hairless cowhide, the unwashed

      covering off a cheap shield; and he used to go
      with baker-women and with rent-boys on the
           make,
       seeking a phoney livelihood.

      His neck was often in the stocks or on the rack,
      his back flogged with a rawhide whip, his hair and
           beard
       plucked out, the 'poor wretch' Artemon.

      And now he wears gold ear-rings, rides about in
           traps,
      'Koisyra's son',* and holds an ivory sunshade up,
       as ladylike as anything.

389   You're a hospitable girl:
      I'm thirsty, let me drink!

390   The lovely-haired daughters of Zeus
      danced lightly there.

391   But now the city's crown of walls is gone.

392   It's not our sort of thing, and not attractive.

393   The vexatious War-god loves the brave . . .

394(a) Delightful, melodious swallow of spring.

394(b) Alexis the Bald is a-wooing again.

395   My temples are grey,
      my hair is white,
         youth's beauty past;

      my teeth rot away;
       life's sweet delight
         not long now can last.

      So I often lament,
       afraid of Hell:
         it's a dreadful tip,

with a grim descent,
   as you know full well
     it's a one-way trip.

396   Bring water, bring wine, boy, bring us wreaths
of flowers: I'm going to spar with Love.

397   And woven
garlands of lotus they hung about their chests.

398   Love's game of fivestones means
frenzy and uproar on earth.

399   Takes off her tunic like a Dorian lass.

400   Once more I took refuge from Love
with Pythomandrus.

401   Putting arm once more
through the Carian-made shield-grip.

402(*a*)   I long to share my youth with you:
you've such an attractive character.

402(*b*)   Love approves of fairness.

402(*c*)   For the lads should like me well
for the things I have to say,
as I sing attractive songs
and can speak attractive words.

403   I'm borne over unmarked reefs.

404   Youth and health.

406   And from it took out a great treasure

407   So give me your slender thighs, dear boy, as a
         toast!

408   . . . her gently, like a tender unweaned fawn
that's left alone in the forest by
its antlered mother, trembling with fright.

409   And in a clean goblet let it be poured,
three parts to five.

410   Let's wreathe our brows with celery
and celebrate the festival
for Dionysus.

411(*a*)   I wish I could die. No other way
out of these troubles can ever be found.

411(b)   Dionysus' loose-hipped Bassarids.

412   And won't you let me go home, now I'm drunk?

413   Once again Love has struck me with his mighty
            axe
          like a smith, and doused me in the icy mountain
            stream.

414   And you've shorn off your soft hair's perfect
            bloom.

415   slinging the Sicilian *kottabos*.*

416   But I hate anyone
          with surly, difficult manners. I have come
          to know that you, Megistes,
          are one of the quiet sort.

417   Thracian filly, why so sharply
          shy away with sidelong glances,
            thinking I've no expertise?

          Be assured, I'd put your bit on
          smartly, hold the reins and run you
            round the limits of the course.

          But for now you graze the meadows,
          frisk and play, for want of any
            good experienced riding man.

418   Hear an old man's prayer,
          maid with the nice hair and the golden dress.

419   Aristoclides, you're the first I mourn of my brave
            friends:
          you lost your young life to defend your land from
            slavery.

420   When I get white hairs mixed among the dark.

421   and my mind is stunned.

422   (Smerdies,) tossing his Thracian mane.

423+S 313
          And lay to rest, O Zeus, that foreign sound,
          in case you(?) talk barbarian-style.

424   and the chamber wherein he
          was not so much the bridegroom as the bride.

425   You seem like gentle visitors, who want
       only a roof and a fire.

427 (*To a woman*)
       And don't keep making burbling sounds
       like a sea-wave as you slurp down
       the equalizer-cup beside
       the canny Gastrodora.

428   Once more I'm in love and not in love,
       once more insane and not insane.

429+*SLG* p. 157
       Whoever wants to fight,
       he's welcome, let him fight.
       But as for me, give here, boy,
       the sweet wine for a toast.

430   You're overdoing it.

431   He doesn't bar the doors and sleep in peace.

432 (*A woman speaks*)
       I'm starting to be wrinkled, over-ripe,
           as a result of your lust.

433   While I held a full cup for Erxion
       the whitecrest, and was working through the
           same.

434   And as for wreaths, each man wore three,
       two rose, the other Naucratis.

435   The tables covered with good things of every
           sort.

436   And stick one's hand in the frying-pan.

437   I run away from her,
       scared as a cuckoo.

439   winding thighs round thighs.

440   ever to see too much; for lots are interested in you.

441(*a*)   and chopped right through the neck.

441(*b*)   and her shift was torn in two.

443   trembles with dark-leaved bay and olive green.

444   Virginal Love
       agleam with longing.

P. Oxy. 3722 fr. 17 ii 7
    Hey! What manner is this?

el. 2 I like him not, who when he drinks by the full
            bowl
        tells only of disputes and tearful war,
    but rather him who blends the Muses' boon with
            Love's,
        and turns his mind to good cheer and delight.

el. 3   What care I, dear friend,
    for the bent-bowed Cimmerians, or the Scythians?

el. 4 I have become a drinker.

LASUS

702   I sing of Demeter and Clymenus' consort, the
            Maid,*
       rousing a honey-cry hymn
       in the low-booming Aeolian mode.

ASIUS

14   There came an aged, crippled, tramp-like branded
         slave,
       a parasite, to Meles' wedding feast,
     all uninvited, wanting broth; while in the midst
       the hero stood, arisen from the mire.

DEMODOCUS

1   The Milesians
aren't fools—it's just that they do foolish things.

2   Another from Demodocus:
        your Lerian is a knavish man—
     not some, but all (save Procleës;
        and even he's a Lerian).

6   If you meet Teians, insist on Prienian justice.

PYTHERMUS

910   Nothing else matters, it seems, apart from gold.

ANANIUS

1   Apollo, who art in Delos, or Pytho, perhaps,
       or Naxos, or Miletus, or in holy Claros,
       come to the festival—or do you want
       to travel all the way to Scythia?

2–3   Of gold, Pythermus states that nothing else
           compares.

       . . . . . .

       If someone locked a lot of gold up in a house
       with two or three people, and a small amount of
           figs,
       he'd soon find out how much more figs are worth
           than gold.

4   And I love you far the best
       of all men, as the cabbage is my witness.

5   In springtime perch is best, in winter maigre;
       of fancy dishes, prawns served on a fig-leaf.
       A kid's nice meat in autumn; pork is right
       at the grape-treading. That's also the time
       for dogfish, sea-hare, and your thresher shark.
       In summer, with the crickets yattering,
       eat lamb; and as for sea-food thenabouts,
       a tunny's no bad snack, indeed it stands
       out among all fish in a savoury sauce.
       And fatted veal, I reckon, 's nice by night or day.

HIPPONAX

1   O Clazomenians, Bupalus has killed . . .

2–2a   She was clad in a Coraxian shift,
       [but bare] as far as the Sindian Gap.

3   He called on Maia's son, Cyllene's sultan.*

3a   'Hermes, watchdog-choker—"Candaules", to put it
          in Lydian—
       comrade of thieves, come and help me pull this
          rope.'

4–4a   Cicon the son of Pandales, the ill-starred mullah
       with his bay wreath . . . this Amythaonid*
       with nothing propitious to foretell.

5   To cleanse the town and be pelted with
          fig-branches.*

6   . . . in winter, pelting him and whipping him
       with fig-branches and squills, just like a scapegoat.

7   He must be adopted as our scapegoat.

8   and place within his reach
       figs, barley-cake, and cheese, like scapegoats eat.

9   They've long been waiting for them,
          open-mouthed,
       armed with fig-branches like they have for
          scapegoats.

10   . . . till he's starved dry; let him be led a scapegoat
       and given seven lashes on the willy.

12   With these words gulling the good folk of
          Erythrae,
       the mother-fucker Bupalus with Ārētē,
       preparing to withdraw the unspeakable skin (?)
          . . .

13   They were drinking from a pail—she had no cup,
       the slave had fallen on to it and smashed it.

14   And from the pail they drank;
now he, and now Ārētē drank a toast.

15   Why have you made your home
with the wretch Bupalus?

16   And I at dusk
went to Ārētē under a lucky heron
and booked in for the night.

17   For Ārētē,
as she bent over for me towards the lamp . . .

19 What birthcord-snipper wiped and cleaned you up,
you blighted creature, as you squirmed and
      mewled?

20 Thinking to whack the first bloke with his stick.

21 He asks half a dollar for pecking at his cock.

22 Knocking her nose out, and the wick as well.

23 Upon these men shall fall a chilling ague.

25 'Artemis damn you!' 'And Apollo damn *you*!'

26–26a For one of them, steadily dining on
tunny and gentleman's relish every day,
just like some eunuch kept at Lampsacus,
ate up the allotment; so I have to dig
the rocky hillside, munching modestly
on a few figs and barley cobs—slaves' feed—
not champing hare and francolin, not I,
not tarting pancakes up with sesame,
or dipping waffles into honeycombs.

27 And if they catch the wogs, they sell them off,
the Phrygians to Miletus to grind corn . . .

28 Shoulder-deep-slackjaw Mimnes, another time
don't paint a snake along a trireme's hull
that's running back from prow to tillerman.
That'll be ruinous, you berk, you nerd,
and a bad omen for the tillerman,
if a snake comes and bites him on the shin!

29a His belly burbling like a pan of soup.

30   I think it's wrong that Critias the Chian
      was seized as an adulterer down there
      in the women's chapel.

32+34 Hermes, dear Hermes, Maia's son, Cyllenian,
      hear thou my prayer, for I am bloody frozen,
      my teeth are chattering . . .
      Grant Hipponax a cloak and a nice tunic
      and some nice sandals and nice fur boots,
      and sixty gold sovereigns to balance me up . . .
      For thou hast never granted me a cloak
      thick in the winter to cure me of the shivers,
      nor hast thou wrapped my feet in thick fur boots
      to stop my chilblains bursting.

35   I'll say, 'Cyllenian Hermes, Maia's son . . .'

36   And Wealth—he's all too blind—he's never come
      to my house, never said, 'Hipponax, here's
      three thousand silver drachmas, and a heap
      of other stuff besides.' No, he's a dimwit.

37   . . . said they should pelt and stone Hipponax.

38   Zeus, father Zeus, Olympian gods' sultan,
      wherefore hast thou not given me gold, silver?

39   I'll see my suffering soul go to damnation
      if you don't send a peck of barley soonest
      so I can use the groats to make myself
      a posset I can take for my wretched state.

40   O Malis, bless me: grant, I pray, that having
      a numbskull master, I don't get a beating.

41   And now he threatens to make me a worthless
          fellow

42   . . . the Smyrna road, straight on
      through Lydia, past the tomb of Attales
      and Gyges' gravestone and Sesostris' column
      and Tos' memorial, sultan at Mytalis,
      turning your paunch towards the setting sun.

44   And if you like, I'll let you have him cheap.

47   With him await the dawn of white-robed day;
      then you'll salaam Phlyesian Hermes, then . . .

48   The dark fig, sister of the vine.

50   He/she lived behind the town in the Smyrna
          district,
      between Roughside and Scabby Edge.

51   Then, smearing along his keel with caulking
          wax . . .

52   But you're holding your cloak wrapped round:
          selling a plover?

53   But straightway yattering at one another . . .

54   A screech-owl, page and herald of the dead.

56   Piercing the jar-lid with a thin pipette.

57   Dripping, like a strainer
      dripping dead wine.

58   And sweet rose-unguent, and a pan of wheat.

59   He sits and warms his blisters by the embers
      incessantly.

60   I wore a wreath of plums and mint.

61   . . . croaked like a jay in the jakes.

62   . . . naked on a bed of straw.

63   And Myson,* whom Apollo
      declared to be the sensiblest man alive.

65   . . . eagerly off the stern-tip into the sea.

66   and doesn't bite afterwards, like a tricksy dog.

67   People who've drunk neat wine don't care a damn.

68   Two days in a woman's life give greatest pleasure:
      those of her wedding and her funeral.

70   . . . (she) grunting . . .
      this godforsaken wretch, who used to poke
      his sleeping mother's sea-anemone . . .
      [May the gods strike him] blind . . . and crippled.

72   Beside his chariot and white Thracian foals
      . . . hard by the walls of Ilios
      Rhesus* was despoiled, the Aeneans' sultan.

73   And he pissed blood and shat a stream of gall,
      while I . . .

All the teeth in my jaws have been dislodged;
I go about . . . I fear . . .

78   . . . he used bad language and . . .
        . . . warm ashes . . .
        but went not in where there was flame or fire.
        Throughout the month of . . . he would go,
        [chewing] dung-beetles, to the Cabiri's shrine
        and [make an offering of] a sprat or two.
        Then, going home, he dined on mulberries,
        and with the juice he dyed this fellow* red
        around the nose, spat on it thrice, and . . .
        shagged off at last . . .

79   . . . this foolishness . . . hitting his jaw
        . . . made them out of (into?) wax . . .
        . . . and splatter-shat upon . . .
        . . . with gold-gleaming wand . . . near the
            bedpost.
        Hermes, escorting him to Hipponax's
        [smuggled] the sneak-thief past the wretched dog
        [that] hisses like a viper [when friends come.]
        . . . Hipponax, taking thought at night
        . . . and devised . . .
        . . . he pondered. To the Appeaser
        [the mulla]h [sacrificed] . . . a fly . . .
        Then with three witnesses he went at once
        to where the bastard has his vino-shop,
        and found a fellow sweeping out the place,
        using a clump of thorn for lack of a broom.

84   On the floor . . . undressing . . .
        we bit and kissed . . .
        keeping a look-out through the doors . . .
        in case . . . should catch us naked . . .
        She was eagerly . . .
        while I was fucking . . .
        pulling out to the tip, like skinning a sausage,
        saying to hell with Bupalus . . .
        Straightway she [pushed] me out, and I [brimmed
            over.]

Now after our exertions we had [rest,]
I . . . like a wrinkled sail . . .

92   She spoke in Lydian:* 'Faskat ikrol'l' —
in Arsish, 'Up the arse . . .',
and [pulling down] my ball by the bal[d patch]
she thrashed me with a fig-branch, like [a
    scapegoat]
fast[ened in] the stocks. And there [I was]
under two torments: on one side the branch
[was killing] me, descending from above,
[my arse on the other] spattering me with shit.
The passage stank; and dung-beetles came buzzing
after the smell, over fifty of them:
some attacked, while others [whet] their te[eth],
and others fell upon the Arsenal doors . . .

104   . . . bending back his fingers . . .
. . . as he squirmed about
. . . I jumped on his belly
. . . lest he should think to curse me
. . . gnashed my teeth and bashed
. . . with legs apart
. . . I took off my cloak
. . . rubbing the dust off my feet
. . . I barred the door
. . . covering up the fire
. . . and lined my nostrils
with perfume . . . as used by Croesus.

. . . to trip his feet.
Slipping, he implored the seven-leafed cabbage
he used to offer potted to Pandora
at the Thargelia,* before the scapegoat.
. . . his forehead and his sides.

114a   May someone pluck his arsehole, soften up . . .

114c   An interprandial pooper.

115   drifting about on the wave.
At Salmydessos* may topknotted Thracian braves
  welcome him naked ashore,

and may he there endure a multitude of woes,
    eating the bread of a slave.
I hope they find him frozen stiff, and from the
      brine
    covered in seaweed and slime,
his teeth a-chatter, like a dog from lack of strength
    lying with face in the sand
right by the water-line, under the breaking waves.
    That's what I'd like to see done
to my betrayer who has trampled on his oaths,
    who was my friend in the past.

117   the cloak . . .
    creel . . . you like
to sit nearby. Hipponax here's aware of this
    better than anyone else,
and Ariphantus knows. I envy those that have
    never yet seen you around,
you dirty stinking thief. Well, you can quarrel with
    potter Aeschylides now:
he's been and carried off your household goods,
    and laid
all your dishonesty bare.

118   O Sannus, as you wear a godless nose
    and can't control your appetite
and have a ravening beak just like a heron's

     .   .   .   .

lend me your ear . . .
    I want to give you some advice.

     .   .   .   .

    Your arms are wasted, and your neck;
and yet you eat up. Careful you don't get
    the gripes . . .
First strip and do your movements; Cicon will
    pipe you the tune of Codalus.

118a   And all his household property's unharmed.

119   If only I could get a girl both beautiful and slender.

120-1   Take my mantle, lads, and let me punch old
      Bupalus in the eye.

     I've got two right hands, you know; I hit the target
        when I punch.

122   Once more I'll have to sue the bastard Metrotimus.

123   and get it better judged than Bias of Priene.

124   and not suck on a Lebedos dried fig from
        Kamandolos.

125   . . . eating bread of Cyprian Amathous wheat.

127   . . . and the daughter of Zeus, Cybebe, and
        Thracian Bendis.

128   Tell me, O Muse,* of Eurymedontiades the
        Charybdis,
     him of the gastric carvers, who eats in irregular
        fashion:
     tell how amid the shingle the wretch will
        wretchedly perish
     by the vote of the people beside the limitless
        seashore.

129   How did he come to Bendova's isle?*

129*a*   Why do you feed me on gamblers?

155   drank it up like a lizard in an alley.

177   Blest Hermes, who both knowest how to wake the
        sleeper
     and how to put to sleep the wakeful . . .

Sixth to Fifth Century

ANONYMOUS THEOGNIDEA

1–4   Lord, son of Leto, child of Zeus, I never will
        forget thee at my outset or my close.
      No, I will sing thee first and last and in between,
        always; so hearken, grant me all success.

5–10 Lord Phoebus, when the lady Leto gave you birth,
        gripping the palm-tree with her slender arms,
      you loveliest of the immortals, by the circle-lake,
        fair Delos was pervaded end to end
      by an ambrosial fragrance, and the vast earth
        smiled,
        and the deep salty white-flecked main rejoiced.

15–18 Muses and Graces, Zeus's daughters who came
        once
        to Cadmus' wedding and sang this fair song:
      'We love what's beautiful, we love not what is
        not.'
      This was the word from your immortal lips.

73–4 Don't even let your friends in on your plans, not
        all:
        only a fraction are reliable.

83–6 Search the whole world, and you'll not find so
        many men
        that you can't get them in a single ship
      who show discretion in their speech and in their
        face
        and are not drawn by greed to wickedness.

87–90+1083–4

Don't speak nice words to me and keep your
    heart elsewhere
if I'm your friend and you're an honest man.
Either be friendly with sincerity, or spurn
    me openly and be an enemy.
That's how a decent man should be towards a
    friend,
    his attitude consistent to the end.

93–4   Whoever compliments you while you're face to face
    but, once apart, gives tongue maliciously,

. . . . . .

95–6   That sort of comrade is by no means to commend
    who speaks smooth-tongued while minded
        otherwise.

97–100   No, may I have the sort of friend who knows his
        friend
    and, even when he's difficult, accepts
    him like a brother. Now take this to heart, my lad,
    and some day you will call me back to mind.

113–14   Don't ever take a rascal for your bosom friend:
    steer clear of him–a bad port in a storm.

155–8   Soul-grinding poverty, accursed indigence—
    never hold these against a man in pique.
    Zeus tilts the balance now to this side, now to that:
    now to be rich, now to be penniless.

161–4   Many are weak of wit but favoured of the gods;
    their prospects that were dismal turn out fair;
    and there are those who plan things wisely, but
        who lack
    heaven's favour, and they toil with no success.

165–6   No man is prosperous, no man is poor, no man
    is low or high, but for the will of heaven.

167–8   We all have different troubles: no man that the sun
    looks down upon is truly fortunate.

169–70   Whom the gods bless, even the captious must
        applaud,
    whereas a man's own effort counts for nought.

171–2   Pray to the gods. Theirs is the power. Without the
             gods
           neither good fortune comes to men nor bad.

193–6   He knows she's of ignoble stock, and yet he takes
             her as his bride, led by the call of wealth.
           Good name and bad name marry; force of
             circumstance,
               which gives a man new standards, grips him
               hard.

197–208 Such wealth as comes from God by way of
             righteousness
               and free from stain, abides for evermore;
           but if a man acquires it wrongly, out of greed,
             or by a false oath takes what is not his,
           at first he thinks he's made a gain, but in the end
             it turns out ill; the gods' design prevails.
           Men get misled, you see, because the Blessed ones
             don't punish sin upon the very act:
           one man may pay his woeful due himself, and not
             leave doom suspended over his dear sons;
           another justice never overtakes, for death
             too soon, uncaring, settles o'er his eyes.

213–14 My heart, display your facets to reflect your friends,
             and blend a temper to accord with each.

215–18 Adopt the cunning of the octopus, who takes
             the aspect of the rock he loiters at.
           Now tag along with this line, now again change
             hue:
               cleverness beats consistency for sure.

221–6   The man who fancies that his neighbour is a fool
             while he alone is crafty and adroit,
           he's unintelligent, his good sense is impaired.
             For all of us alike have crafty thoughts,
           but one man doesn't care to chase dishonest gains,
             another favours treachery and tricks.

255–6   The finest thing is what's most right; the best is
             health;
               the nicest is to get the thing one craves.

257–60   I'm a fine horse, a winner, but a scoundrel's now
               my jockey—this it is that pains me most.
           Many a time I've thought of breaking off the bit,
               throwing my worthless rider, running free.

261–2   No wine for me: beside my slender girl a man
               not half my worth is having all the fun.

263–6   Her mum and dad must like their wine well
                   cooled: she comes
               so often to the well, and draws, and cries—
           the well by which I took her round the waist, and
                   kissed
               her on the neck, while prettily she squealed.

267–70   You all know Poverty, pariah though she be;
               she visits not the courts or market-place,
           for everywhere she's elbowed, everywhere
                   abhorred,
               and hated everywhere she shows her face.

271–8   All other things the gods have given mortal men
               in equal shares—accursed age, and youth—
           but what is worst of all in human life—not death
               nor any sickness is so hard to bear—
           is when you raise your sons and give them all they
                   need,
               providing for them with much sacrifice,
           and then they hate their father, praying for his
                   death,
               and shun him like some beggar at the door.

279–82   A knave will likely have a knave's morality,
               not caring what resentment he provokes.
           A scoundrel has so many opportunities
               for easy crime, and thinks he's got it made.

283–6   Trust no one in this town in any step you take,
               whatever pledge of friendship he has sworn—
           not even if he seeks to make the mighty king
               of the immortals, Zeus, his guarantor.

287–92   In such a town of grumblers nothing's ever right.
               Well, there are always many out of luck;

but now the gentry's troubles fill the lower class
   with glee, and they exult in uncouth ways.
All inhibition's gone, and brazen lawlessness,
   defeating justice, holds the land in sway.

293–4   Not even the lion always feasts on meat. For all
      his strength, he's sometimes caught in helpless
        plight.

295–8   It's a hard burden for a chatterbox to hold
      his tongue; but when he talks, he is a bore.
    Nobody likes him, and it's not from choice one
        goes
      to join that sort of man's symposium.

301–2   Be nasty and be nice, be gracious and be gruff
      to slaves and servants and the folk next door.

303–4   Don't meddle with the good life, leave it
        undisturbed,
      but change the bad one till you've set it
        straight.

305–8   Not every villain is a villain from the womb:
      it's only after making friends with knaves
    they learn bad ways and ugly talk and lawlessness,
      believing everything their comrades say.

309–12   In company a man should keep his counsel, seem
      to notice nothing, almost not be there,
    just joke and banter. Then, when he goes out, he
        knows
      what each man's like, and this can be his
        strength.

313–14   When it's a rave-up, then I damn well rave; but
        when
      it's serious, I'm the seriousest of all.

332*ab*   An exile has no friend he can depend upon.
      That's the most painful thing about his plight.

341–50   Olympian Zeus, fulfil my prayer, the time is ripe:
      against my ills now grant me something good,
    or let me die, if I find no relief from these
      sore troubles. Let me repay hurt with hurt:

it's only fair. Yet I see no revenge in sight
    on those who've robbed me of my house and
       home
and made me play the dog that crossed the icy
       stream
    in winter flood and shook it all straight off.
I'd like to drink their blood! May my good fairy
       come
    and do all this exactly to my taste.

351–4   O wretched Poverty, why won't you up and seek
       another man? Don't cling, I love you not,
    so go away, call at another house. Don't stay
       to share this miserable life with me.

363–4   Flatter your foe well. When he's eating from your
       hand,
    then get your own back. No need to explain.

365–6   Keep your thoughts back, and let your tongue be
       ever smooth.
    Quick temper is a mark of low-class men.

373–400   Dear Zeus, I'm quite surprised at you. You're king
       of all,
    the power and the glory's yours alone;
you understand the heart and mind of every man,
    and yours, lord, is the highest majesty.
So how, Zeus, can you bring yourself to treat alike
    wrongdoers and the law-abiding man,
whether we are disposed to sensible restraint
    or give way to unrighteousness and crime?
Are there no guidelines set by heaven for mortal
    men,
    no path to follow that will please the gods?

                     .   .

    [Some people rob and steal quite
       shamelessly,]
but still succeed and prosper: others, who refrain
    from wicked acts, preferring what is right,
get only poverty, whose child is helplessness,
    who blights men's wits by force of circumstance

and leads their hearts astray to do some wrong. A man
  puts up perforce with much indignity,
beaten by indigence, from which he learns bad ways
  despite himself: deceit and trickery
and quarrelling. No other ill compares with this,
  for it produces utter helplessness.
In poverty, when want takes hold, it's soon made clear
  who is a rogue and who's a decent sort.
The one has honest thoughts, the man within whose breast
  the attitudes are planted always straight,
whereas the other shows no sense, come good or ill,
  while the good man is forced to deal with both,
treat friends with due respect, shun ruinous perjury
  . . . .
  . . . .
  with care, avoiding the immortals' wrath.

401–6 Don't strive too hard. Due measure's best for everything
  in human life. Often a man strives hard
for status, seeking gain—a man whom God intends
  to lead astray into great wrongfulness,
and easily makes bad appear to him as good,
  and worthwhile things appear to him as bad.

407–8 You were my best friend, but you've fallen short. No fault
  of mine: it's your own attitude that's wrong.

413–14 I'll not become so fortified, or let the wine
  so bring me on, that I speak ill of you.

415–18 I search, but can discover no one like myself
  to be my true friend, pure of all deceit.
Apply the touchstone, rub me down like gold with lead:
  surface and inside tell a single tale.

419–20   There's much I understand but let pass by,
               perforce
         silent, aware how little we can do.

421–4   Many men have no shutters on their mouths that
               fit
         correctly, and there's much they're careless of.
         Often there's bad inside that's best left stored
               away;
         it's better something good comes out than bad.

425–8   Best thing of all for men is simply not be born
               and never look upon the keen sun's light;
         but when you're born, best pass as soon as
               possible
         death's door, and lie with earth heaped thick
               above.

439–40   He's foolish, who keeps watch on my propensities
               and meanwhile takes no steps to guard his own.

441–6   For no one's wholly fortunate. The man of worth
               puts up with ill, but doesn't let it show;
         the no-good lacks the art of standing firm, come
               good
         or ill, with spirit. The immortals' gifts
         come to us in all shapes and sorts. We must
               endure
         and take whatever the immortals send.

447–52   Or wash me down: the water will run steadily
               quite clean and unpolluted off my head.
         In everything you'll find me like refiner's gold,
               still showing yellow where the touchstone rubs.
         Upon its surface no dark tarnishing or rust
               takes hold; it keeps its brightness ever pure.

453–6   If you'd as much brains, mate, as you've stupidity,
               if you'd as much sense as you've senselessness,
         you'd be looked up to by as many in this town
               as now consider you a useless prat.

457–60   A young wife does not suit a husband who is old:
               the boat will not obey the steering-oar;

she slips her anchor, breaks her mooring-ropes,
    and oft
she finds another harbour for the night.

461–2   Don't fix your heart and mind on unattainable
        designs: it never gets you anywhere.

463–4   The gods give nothing easy, neither good nor bad.
        It's hard endeavours that they most exalt.

465–6   Work for high standards, be a friend of
        righteousness,
        and don't give way to ignoble avarice.

497–8   The witless and the sound of wit alike
        turn empty-headed when they drink too deep.

499–502 Of gold and silver, experts make assay by fire,
        but wine is what shows up the heart of man,
    even a clever fellow, when he drinks too deep,
        bringing his wisdom into disrepute.

503–8   I'm heavy-headed with wine, Onomacritus, not
        any longer
    in control of my mind; drink has me on the
        retreat.
    Here is the room going round and round. I'd
        better try standing,
    find out whether the wine's also got hold of my
        legs
    and of my innermost wits. I'm afraid I'll do
        something silly
    in my fortified state, badly disgracing myself.

509–10 Wine drunk too copious is a bane, but if it's drunk
        with prudence, then no bane, but sheerest boon.

511–22 You've come then, Clearistus, crossed the deep
        blue sea.
    You're broke, old mate, I know; and so am I;
    but I'll bring out the best of what I've got, and if
        a friend of yours turns up, couch how you like.
    I won't hide anything that's in the house, nor fetch
        in extra stocks for entertaining you.
    As for provisioning your ship, I will provide
        as best I can and as the gods allow;

and if they ask about my way of life, reply
  'Poor, by good standards, but by poor ones,
    good:
if one old house-friend visits, he won't let him
  down,
  but entertaining more's beyond his means.'

523–6   It's not for nothing, Wealth, that men esteem you
        most,
      for you make light of dismal circumstance.
    Besides, to have wealth is the proper mark of class,
      while poverty's the burden of the prole.

527–8   I sing alas for youth, alas for curst old age—
      the approach of one, the passing of the other.

529–30 Nor have I friend or trusty comrade e'er betrayed,
      and in my soul there's nothing of the slave.

531–4   My heart within me's always gladdened when I
        hear
      the reed-pipes sounding out with lovely voice.
    I'm happy drinking well and singing to the pipes,
      I'm happy fingering the clear-toned lyre.

535–8   The slave can never hold his head up straight:
      it's always crooked, and his neck is bent.
    For rose and hyacinth grow not from squills,
      nor from slave mother child with spirit free.

547–8   Pressure no man with roughness, let fair dealing
        serve:
      there's nothing stronger than a kindly act.

555–60 A man laid low in grievous troubles must endure
      and ask the immortal gods for his release.
    Take heed: your fortune's balanced on a razor's
        edge:
      sometimes you will have plenty, sometimes
        less,
    which means you'll never get to be a millionaire,
      but never sink too deep in poverty.

561–2   I pray to have some for myself, and give my
        friends
      the surplus—from my enemies' estates.

563–6 Get asked to dine, and seat yourself beside a man
        of worth, who's mastered every kind of skill.
      When he says something clever, note it, so you
        learn
      and have this bit of profit to take home.

567–70 I sport and make the most of youth; for when I die
        it's long enough I'll lie there like a stone,
      reduced to silence, lovely sunshine left behind,
        blind evermore, fine fellow that I am.

571–2 Vain fantasy's no good, experience is the thing.
        Many imagine joys they've never known.

573–4 Do good, receive good: why send other courier?
        Doing a good turn speeds your message straight.

575–6 My friends betray me—for I steer clear of my foe
        as helmsmen steer clear of the hidden reef.

577–8 'It's easier to make good bad than make bad good.'
        —Don't try to teach me. I'm too old to learn.

579–82 I loathe a knave, I draw my veil and pass him by,
        a creature with a small bird's empty brains;
      and I loathe a roving woman, or a reckless man
        who wants to plough another fellow's field.

583–4 But what's already happened cannot be
        undone. What's yet to come is what to watch.

591–4 One must endure whate'er the gods give mortal
        men,
      and yet not make too much of either lot:
      in bad times not too heartsick, nor when things look
        up
      straightway exulting, till the outcome's clear.

595–8 Let's go on being friends, mate, at a distance though.
        One can have too much of anything, bar wealth.
      Yes, let's be friends, long-term, but stick with other
        blokes
      who better understand what makes you tick.

599–602 I saw you—straying down the same old common
        road
      you used to, cheating on my love for you.

To hell with you, whom gods detest and men can't
trust,
  whose bosom held a cold and cunning asp.

603–4 Magnesia was destroyed by lawlessness like this
  that now pervades this holy town of ours.

605–6 Surplus has ruined far more men than deficit—
  all those that wanted more than was their due.

607–10 There's small joy when a lie's first told, and in the
end
  the gain it brings is foul, contemptible.
There's nothing fine or fair about it, once a lie
  attends a man and issues from his lips.

611–14 To find fault isn't hard, no more than praising is;
  it's paltry men that turn their minds to it.
Paltry men, paltry chatter; they won't hold their
tongues;
  but gentlemen know where to draw the line.

615–16 There's not a single good and reasonable man
  of all the sun today looks down upon.

617–18 By no means everything turns out as men desire:
  the immortals' power surpasses ours by far.

619–22 All sick at heart I toss and turn in helplessness;
  I haven't cleared poverty's rocky point.
They all respect a rich man, and despise the poor;
  in everyone the attitude's the same.

623–4 There's every kind of ill in men, and every kind
  of excellence, and ways of making do.

625–6 It's hard for a man of sense to talk at length with
fools,
  and hard for him always to hold his tongue.

627–8 It's bad form to be drunk in sober company,
  or to stay sober when the rest are drunk.

629–30 The prime of youth and vigour goes with empty
brains;
  it oft emboldens men to go astray.

633–4 Think over twice or thrice what comes into your
head.
  An over-hasty man's disaster-prone.

635-6 Good judgement and discretion cling to men of
      worth;
      but these are now a real minority.

637-8 Danger and hope are two of a kind in human life:
      unmanageable forces, both of them.

639-40 It's often so, that men's designs run well, past hope
       and promise, yet are crowned with no success.

641-4 You'll never know who is your friend or who your
      foe
      until you find yourself in serious straits.
      Plenty are pals and comrades when the drinking's
      on,
      but not so many when the going's tough.

645-6 You'll not find many patrons to be trusty friends
      when you're in helpless plight, cast down at heart.

647-8 Now inhibition is extinct in human life,
      and brazenness is rampant everywhere.

649-52 Vile Poverty, why must my shoulders bear your
       weight
       that so deforms my body and my soul?
       You teach me many an ugly trick despite myself
       and all I know of good society.

657-66 Be not too vexed by hardships, nor when fortune's
       fair
       too joyful. Men of worth should take what comes.
       Don't ever swear that such and such will never be:
       the gods resent it, and the outcome's theirs.
       They act, what's more: bad fortune is transformed to
       good
       and good to bad; a man in penury
       grows quickly rich, or one who has abundant wealth
       loses it all within a single night;
       a wise man goes astray, a fool's imaginings
       come true; even the no-good wins respect.

683-6 Many are rich but stupid; others strive for good
      but are oppressed by arduous poverty.
      And both these sorts are helpless to achieve their
      aims,
      the second barred by means, the first by wit.

687–8 It is not granted unto men to fight the gods,
        or to pass judgement: no one has this right.

689–90 One ought to cause no harm, except when harm
            were due,
        nor do such deeds as are not better done.

691–2 *Bon voyage*, Chaeron, o'er the mighty sea, and may
        Poseidon bring you safe to cheer your friends.*

693–4 Surplus has been the ruin of many a foolish man:
        when you're well off, it's hard to draw the line.

695–6 My heart, I cannot give you everything to suit:
        you're not the only one to crave what's nice.

697–718

        When I fare well, I've friends enough; but if some ill
            befalls me, few can be relied upon.
        To most men's way of thinking, only one thing
            counts:
            that's wealth, and nothing else is any use,
        not even if you've Rhadamanthys' prudent head,
            or brains to beat the Aeolid Sisyphus,*
        who by his wits returned even from Hades' house
            with sly persuasion of Persephone,
        who brings oblivion and impairs men's
            consciousness.
        That no one else has ever yet contrived,
        once death's dark cloud's enfolded him and he has
            gone
        into the shadowed country of the dead
        and passed the gates of blackness that shut in the
            souls
            of the deceased, for all that they protest.
        Even from there the hero Sisyphus returned
            up to the sunlight by his cleverness.
        Nor does it help if you can tell convincing lies
            and speak with godlike Nestor's nimble tongue,
        or run more swiftly than the speeding Harpies* go
            and the fleet-footed sons of Boreas.
        No, everyone must just agree on this, that wealth
            with all men has the greatest influence.

729–30 Man was assigned to Cares, whose wings are
          many-hued;
       they cry for thought of life and livelihood.

731–52 O father Zeus, I wish the gods could so agree
          that sinners could choose lawlessness, and set
       their hearts on misdemeanour, but that anyone
          who did so, heedless of the gods' regard,
       should pay the price in person, and the father's sins
          should not remain to persecute his sons;
       and that a bad man's sons who fear your anger, Zeus,
          holding themselves to righteous thoughts and
            deeds,
       and in their dealings always cleave to righteousness,
          should never pay for fathers' trespasses.
       That's what I wish the gods approved. But as things
          are,
       the rogue escapes, another takes the rap.
       Again, how is it fair, lord of the deathless gods,
          that someone who keeps out of wrongfulness,
       guilty of no transgression and no perjury,
          a righteous man, suffers unrighteously?
       Who else thereafter, when he looks on this man's
          fate,
       will fear the gods, and in what frame of mind,
       when an unrighteous criminal who takes no care
          to avoid the wrath of any man or god
       commits his crimes and rolls in riches, while the
          good
       are sore oppressed by arduous poverty?

753–6 Take this to heart, my friend, and make wealth
          honestly,
       be sensible, keep clear of lawlessness.
       Never forget these lines, and in the end you will
          be glad you've followed sensible advice.

757–64 May Zeus in heaven always keep his right hand held
          over this town, protecting it from harm;
       also the other blest immortal gods; and may
          Apollo guide my tongue and mind aright.

Let lyre and pipes play on, voicing the holy song,
　　while we with due libations to the gods
keep drinking, making pleasant talk among
　　　ourselves,
　　completely fearless of this Median war.*

765–8 Grant things may be like this, or better, while we
　　　pass
　　our time with cheerful hearts and free from cares
in pleasure. Keep away all bad contingencies,
　　accurst old age, and death's finality.

769–72 The Muses' page and mouthpiece, should he know
　　　some choice
　　invention, must not keep it to himself,
but muse, in turn display, in turn compose again.
　　How will it help him, if it isn't shared?

773–88 Lord Phoebus, you're the one that built the citadel
　　on Pelops' son Alcathous' behalf:*
now keep the Medes' rampaging army off the town,
　　so that the people with a cheerful heart
when spring arrives can make fine hecatomb-parades,
　　enjoying happy feasting and the lyre
and dances round your altar with glad paean-cries.
　　The fact is, I'm afraid when I behold
the ruinous, stupid quarrels of the Greeks; so you
　　look kindly, Phoebus, guard this town of ours.
For me, I've travelled in my time to Sicily,
　　and to Euboea's vine-producing plains,
and handsome Sparta by Eurotas' reedy banks,
　　and I was always kindly entertained;
yet none of all those places gratified my heart—
　　it's true, you know, there is no place like home.

789–94 I want no other interest but high-class life
　　and intellectual culture. Keeping this
I hope to stay enjoying lyre and dance and song,
　　and with the best set keep the best in mind,
doing no wrong or harm to any, citizen
　　or alien, but living righteously.

797–8 Some carp at men of worth, others approve of them:
　　the lower class aren't spoken of at all.

799–800   There's no one born on earth with whom no fault is
               found.
           It's best with fewest people paying heed.

801–4   There never was nor ever will be born a man
               who pleases everyone throughout his life.
           Not even Kronos' son, Zeus, king of gods and men,
               succeeds in satisfying everyone.

823–4   Don't feed a tyrant's power, led by hopes of gain;
               but don't swear by the gods to cause his death.

825–30   How can you bring yourselves to sing songs to the
               pipes?
           You see the frontier from the market-place
           that bounds the land that feeds you as you feast
               away
           with crimson garlands on your golden hair.
           Come, crop this hair short, Scythian, end the revelry,
           lament the loss of our fair-scented land.

831–2   By trusting I lost all, by mistrust kept it safe;
               but neither line is easy to sustain.

837–40   Wretched mankind's beset by two dire fates in drink:
               crippling thirst, and horrid drunkenness.
           I'll steer midway between the two: you won't induce
               me not to drink, nor yet to drink too much.

841–2   Wine's mostly nice to me, save when it leads me on,
               all fortified, to face my enemy.

843–4   But when he that was higher comes to be below,*
               at that time drink no more and hie you home.

845–6   A man well placed is easy to displace again,
               but to make good what's badly placed is hard.

847–50   Trample this empty-witted people down, apply
               the sharp goad, lay on them the heavy yoke.
           You'll find no people so in love with tyranny
               in any land the sun looks down upon.

851–2   May Zeus the Olympian smite the man who
               blandishes
           with soft words, seeking to deceive his friend.

853-4   I knew already, but I know much better now,
             that scoundrels are devoid of gratitude.

855-6   Often this city through its leaders' knavishness
             has run alongshore like a listing ship.

857-60   If one among my friends sees me in some distress,
             he turns his head and will not even look;
         but if some good befalls me—rare thing for a man—
             then everywhere it's hugs and fond regards.

861-4 (*A woman speaks*)
         My near ones let me down, deny me anything
             when male guests come. Then of my own accord
         I leave the hall at evening and return at dawn,
             the hour when the cocks awake and crow.

865-8   To many a worthless man God grants prosperity
             that brings no profit either to his friends
         or him, whereas a real man's glory never dies:
             a spearman's the salvation of his land.

869-72   May the broad brazen sky above crash down on me,
             the fate men used to fear in ancient times,
         if I don't stand by those who show themselves my
             friends,
             and vex and irritate my enemies.

873-6   I praise you, wine, on some points, and find fault
             with some;
             I cannot give you total love or hate.
         You're bane and blessing. Who could criticize you,
             who,
             that has an ounce of expertise, approve?

877-8   Be young, my heart, have fun: soon other men will
             take
             my place, and I'll be dark dust in my grave.

879-84   This wine I'm serving comes from Mount Taygetus.
             My vineyard there was planted on the slopes
         below the summit by old Theotimos, whom
             the gods love; and he dug a cooling stream
         from Platanistous. Drink! It will disperse your cares;
             with this to line you, you'll be much refreshed.

885–6 May peace and plenty rule the town, so we can all
make merry. I've no love of cruel war.

887–8 Don't strain your ears to catch the herald's bawled
commands;
it's not our own land that we're fighting for.

889–90 But it is shaming, when you're on the spot and
horsed,
to get no sighting of the tearful fray.

891–4 O shameful feebleness! Cerinthus is destroyed,
Lelantum's good vine-plain they're ravaging;
the men of worth are exiled, rascals rule the town.
May Zeus wipe out the clan of Cypselus!*

901–2 One man is better, one is worse: each has his role,
as no one man is skilled at everything.

903–30 He who takes care to spend according to his means
is best regarded by discerning men.
For if one could descry the end of life, how far
one had to go before one passed away,
it would make sense for someone who had more time
left
to spend less, so he kept enough to live.
But no, it can't be done. This causes me much grief,
it stings me to the quick, I'm in two minds,
I'm standing at a junction, with two ways ahead,
and I'm deliberating which to choose:
to cut all spending and exist in misery,
or to have fun, achieving nothing much.
I've seen a man who wouldn't spend and never gave
his belly decent food, though rich enough,
but he went down to Hades sooner than he'd planned,
and all his riches went to who knows who;
so that means misplaced pains, and choice of heir
denied.
I've seen another who indulged himself,
used up his wealth, said, 'I'll have fun before I go'—
and now he begs off any friend he sees.
So, Democles, the best of all plans is to match
expenditure to means, and keep account.

Then no one else will share your earnings, if you die,
    and you won't end a beggar and a slave.
However old you grow, your means won't all run
        out;
    and when you're old, that's when you most need
        means,
    for if you're well off, then you've friends enough; if
        not,
    they're few; you're not the fine chap that you were.

931–2   It's wise to save, for nobody will even mourn
        your death unless he sees there's property.

933–8   Few men combine impressive looks with quality:
        how fortunate is one who has them both!
    By everyone he's honoured; all make way for him,
        the young, the old, and those of his own age;
    he grows old in celebrity, and no one thinks
        to cheat him of his due respect and rights.

939–42 I cannot sing in pure tones like the nightingale:
        I went out merrymaking last night too.
    I will not blame the piper either. No, my friend
        (who's musical enough) has let me down.

943–4   I'll stand up here close by the piper, on his right,
        and sing, with prayers to the immortal gods.

945–6   I shall go by the rule, dead straight, and veering off
        to neither side. My judgement must be sound.

947–8   I will adorn my shining city; I'll not let
        the mob take over, or give way to rogues.

949–54 I had a deer's fawn, like a lion in my might,
        caught in my claws, and did not drink its blood;
    I scaled high city walls, and did not sack the town;
        I yoked two steeds, and did not mount the car;
    achieved, left unachieved; fulfilled, did not fulfil;
        performed, performed not; did, and did not do.

955–6   Doing good turns to villains hits you two ways on:
        you lose a pile, and get no gratitude.

957–8   If you've had some big boon from me and shown no
        thanks,
    I hope you'll come in need another time.

959–62 So long as I was drinking from the spring's dark
      flow,
    its water, as I thought, was sweet and good.
  But now it's dirty, other waters running in:
    I'll leave this sewer, find another spring.

963–70 Don't ever praise a man until you know for sure,
    his temperament, his style, his turn of mind.
  Many conceal a false and knavish character,
    adopt a disposition for the day;
  but Time brings their true natures to the light for
      sure.
    Why, I myself was grievously misled,
  approving you too soon, before I got to know
    your many ways. Now I steer clear of you.

971–2 A drinker's party prize—what merit lies in that?
    Often a no-good beats a man of worth.

973–8 No man whom once the earth has covered, who has
      gone
    down to the dark, Persephone's abode,
  has any pleasure listening to lyre or pipes,
    or raising to his lips the wine-god's gift.
  In view of which, I'll give my heart a good time,
    while
    my legs are spry, my head undoddery.

979–82 Give me a man who's friend in deed, not just in
      word,
    who'll make an effort, fight, draw on his funds,
  not one whose talk beguiles me while the drinking's
    on,
    but one who'll act to show what good he is.

983–8 But now let us commit our hearts to festiveness,
    while the delights of pleasure still run on.
  Our youth, our splendour passes by swift as a
      thought:
    not even charging horses go so fast,
  that bear their warrior master madly to the fray,
    galloping blithe across the fertile plain.

989–90   Drink when they're drinking; if you're ever sick
                  at heart,
             let no man notice that you feel oppressed.

991–2   Sometimes you'll be the victim hurt, sometimes
                  the glad
             accomplisher. Man's power comes and goes.

993–1002

             Just set us, Academus, to compete in song,
                  and let there be a boy in choicest bloom
             for prize, as you and I contest in artistry:
                  you'd soon see how the mule excels the ass.
             The Sun in heaven would have brought his steeds
                  upon
                  the level stretch, the mid-part of the day;
             we would be finishing our meal, just as we chose,
                  treating ourselves to every kind of dish,
             and then a pretty Spartan girl with slender hands
                  would clear the wash-jug, fetch the garlands in.

1007–12   Let me advise the world: so long as you possess
                  youth's lovely bloom, and still are sound of mind,
             use what you have for pleasure. No return to youth
                  is granted by the gods to mortal men,
             and no escape from death. Ugly, accursed age
                  takes hold on top, and cuts through our pretence.

1013–16   O happy, lucky man, that finds his way below
                  to Death's dark hall without torment and trial,
             not having had to cower from his foes, perforce
                  transgress, or test the mettle of his friends.

1023–4   I'll never bow my neck beneath my foes' hard yoke,
                  even with Tmolus* pressing on my head.

1029–36   Endure, my heart, even the unendurable:
                  it's only lesser men give way to pique.
             Don't add to your indignity and hurt with boasts
                  you can't make good, embarrassing your friends
             and making your enemies laugh. A mortal man
                  cannot
                  lightly evade the destiny God sends,

either by diving to the purple ocean's bed
or when he's caught in misty Tartarus.

1039–40 O foolish, witless mortals, they that do not fill
the wine-cups when the Dog-star's season starts.

1041–2 Here with the piper! Where our enemy makes
moan
we'll laugh and drink, exulting in his woes.

1043–4 Let's sleep, and leave the gods to guard the town,
our lovely homeland rich in fertile soil.

1045–6 By God, however well wrapped up these fellows
sleep,
they'll jump to let us merrymakers in!

1047–8 For now, let's talk of good things, drink, enjoy
ourselves:
what happens after is the gods' affair.

1049–54 Just like a father to a son I'll give you good
advice; it's up to you to take it in.
Don't ever come to grief by rushing things. Reflect
deeply beforehand, use your own good sense.
It's madmen that have thoughts that fly away with
them;
reflection leads to sense and benefit.

1055–8 But let us talk no more of that. Play me the pipes,
we'll take the Muses up, the two of us.
It's thanks to them we're so well gifted, you and I,
and so well known all round the villages.

1059–62 Often, Timagoras, it's hard, however skilled
you are, to judge a character by looks.
Some keep their worthlessness disguised by
affluence,
and some their worth by cursed poverty.

1063–8 In youth you're free to sleep the night beside a
friend
and satisfy your craving for delight;
you're free to go carousing, singing to the pipes.
There are no pleasures to compare with these

for men and women. Wealth, respect, what use
    are they?
Pleasure beats everything, and jollity.

1069–70 O foolish, witless mortals, weeping for the dead
    but not the fading of the flower of youth.

1073–4 Now tag along with this line, now again change
    hue:
cleverness even beats nobility.

1075–8 When something's still in train, it's very hard to
    tell
what outcome God intends to bring about;
it's veiled in darkness, and until the destined hour
    men cannot see beyond their helplessness.

1079–80 No foe of mine who's worthy will I vilify,
    nor compliment a friend when he's a knave.

1085–6 You're often hard to take, Demonax. It's because
    you've never learned to do things you dislike.

1087–90 Castor and Polydeuces, you that have your home
in Sparta by Eurotas' flowing stream:
send ill on me that e'er I plot against a friend,
    and on him twice the ill he plans for me.

1091–4 My heart has problems where your friendship is
    concerned:
I can't quite hate you, and I can't quite love.
I find that when a man's a friend, it's hard to hate,
    but hard to love, when he is contrary.

1097–1100
Now I take wing and soar free, like a bird that breaks
the knavish trapper's noose and flies away
from off the lake. You've lost my friendship, and
    in time
you'll recognize how sensible I was.

1105–6 When they apply the touchstone, rub you down
    with lead,
you'll prove pure gold, perfect to every eye.

1107–8 O misery! Now by my misfortune I have brought
    joy to my foes and trouble to my friends.

1115–16 You're rich; because I'm poor you taunt me; yet I
               have
             something, and with God's help I'll yet earn
               more.

1117–18 Wealth, handsomest and most alluring of the gods,
             with you even a bum becomes a gent.

1119–22 Give me my span of youth; Apollo love me well,
             fair Leto's son, and Zeus the immortals' king,
           so I may live in goodness, out of all harm's way,
             with youth and affluence to warm my heart.

1123–8   Ah, don't remind me. I've been through
               Odysseus' trials,
             who came up from the mighty house of Death,
           and then with satisfaction, merciless, he slew
             the suitors of Penelope his bride,
           who long had stayed beside her son, awaiting him
             while he explored earth's fearsome fastnesses.

1129–32 I'll drink my fill, ignore soul-grinding poverty
             and hateful fellows that speak ill of me;
           but I lament my lovely youth that's running out,
             and weep at the approach of grim old age.

1135–50 Hope is the only good god now among mankind:
             the rest have left us and gone off to heaven.
           The mighty goddess Trust is gone, Restraint is
               gone,
             and Charity's departed from the earth.
           No longer can you trust in men's judicial oaths,
             and nobody respects the immortal gods;
           the moral man's a vanished breed; morality
             and ancient law are recognized no more.
           But while a man still lives and sees the sun still
               shine,
             if he's religious, let him look to Hope.
           Let him pray to the gods and burn his offerings
             honouring Hope in first place and in last.
           But let him always guard against the crooked lies
             of bad men who, with no heed of the gods,
           direct their thoughts at other people's property
             in foul conspiracy of wickedness.

1151–2 Never forsake the friend you have and seek
            another,
         gulled by the arguments of good-for-noughts.

1153–4 I pray to live in wealth, away from vexing cares,
            doing no harm and suffering no ill.

1155–6 I crave no riches, pray not for them. May I live
            from modest means, just suffering no ill.

1157–60 Riches and cleverness are men's great conquerors:
            riches can never glut your appetite;
         and none, however clever, shuns more cleverness—
            he craves it, and he cannot get enough.

1160*ab* Buy yourself someone new. This I don't have to
            do:
         be grateful for the things I've done before.

1163–4 Keen-witted men have eyes and tongue and ears
            and thought
         all rooted in the middle of their breast.

1165–6 Consort with men of worth, and never mix with
            knaves,
         until your trade's done and you're safely
            home.

1167–8 Good men make good response, and match it by
            their deeds;
         the weak word of the knave's gone with the
            wind.

1169–70 Bad company has bad effects, as you'll find out:
         they're mighty gods that you have sinned
            against.

1181–2 When it's an autocrat, who chews the people up,
         bed him down how you like: the gods don't
            mind.

1185–6 The brain's a good thing; so's the tongue; but they
            are found
         in few men who can keep them both in check.

1187–90 No price you pay can buy escape from death, or
            grim
         misfortune, if its destined end's not nigh,

nor from distress of mind, when God sends pain
    and woe:
    a mortal man cannot get off through bribes.

1191–4 I crave not to be laid upon a kingly couch
    in death: no, give me comfort while I live.
    Thorns make as good a bed as satins for a corpse.
    Hard or soft, it's all the same to him.

1195–6 Swear no false oath upon the immortals. There's
    no way
    of hiding from the gods the debt you owe.

1203–6 I shan't go there, I shan't invite him here,
    nor mourn the tyrant even at his grave,
    no more than he would care if I were dead,
    or let a warm tear trickle from his eye.

1207–8 You're not excluded, and we're not inviting you.
    We like you here, we like you when you're not.

1209–10 A Dusky I was born, but by the walls of Thebes
    I dwell, far sundered from my native land.

1211–16 Don't frivolously mock my parents, Argyris.
    You have been taken into slavery;
    I've much else to complain of, woman, being now
    an exile, but I'm not a wretched slave,
    and I'm not bought and sold. I too can boast a fine
    home town—it lies on the Lethaean Plain.*

1229–30 For I'm called home now by a carcass of the sea*
    that e'en in death speaks through a living
    mouth.

Love poems

1231–4 Cruel Eros, madness-spirits nursed you from your
    birth.
    Because of you* was Ilios brought low,
    and Aegeus' son, great Theseus, and Oïleus' son,
    the noble Ajax, through his foolishness.

1235–8 Lad, change your mind and hear me. It's no
    odious
    or charmless thing I want to tell your heart;

so bring yourself to take my message in: you're not
    compelled to do what isn't to your taste.

1239–40 They'll often tell me foolish tales concerning you,
    and you concerning me; but pay no heed.

1241–2 You'll have fond memories of your past love; of
        the one
    coming along you won't have such control.

1243–4 Yes, let's be friends, long-term; but stick with
            other chaps:
    your tricksy nature turns faith back to front.

1245–6 Water and fire will never mix, and you and I
    will never to each other be true friends.

1247–8 Think on your error and my hate, and be assured
    I'll punish your offence as best I can.

1249–52 Lad, like a horse that's had its fill of barleycorns
        you've found your way back to my stableyard.
    You missed your skilful charioteer, the lovely
        mead,
    the cool spring water, and the shady trees.

1255–6 Whoever does not love lads, horses, hounds,
    must have a heart that never knows good cheer.

1257–8 My lad, you're like the roaming perils that beset
    our life, and cleave to ever different men.

1259–62 My lad, you're good to look at, but upon your
        head
    there sits an obdurate, unfeeling crown.
    You have the disposition of a wheeling kite,
    and let yourself be led by other men.

1263–6 My lad, you have repaid your benefactor ill,
    and shown no gratitude for kindnesses.
    You've never done me any good, but many times
    I've treated you well, yet got no respect.

1267–70 Lads have a horse's outlook. When the charioteer
        lies in the dust, the horse makes no lament:
    he serves the next man who will stuff him full of
        oats.
    The same with lads, they love whoever's by.

1271-4 Lad, your reckless behaviour destroyed my
    sensible instincts,
  and our friends were ashamed, knowing about
    the affair.
  But for a little while you cooled my fever; my
    speeding
    voyage into the night briefly found haven from
    storm.

1275-8 Love too comes up in season, just when earth
    waxes and burgeons with the flowers of spring.
  Then from the beauteous isle of Cyprus Love
    goes forth among mankind to sow his seeds.

1279-82 I won't do ill by you, not even if that is
    my best bet *vis-à-vis* the gods, dear lad.
  They are no small offences that I'm saddled with,
    but lovely lads . . . wronging . . .

1283-94 Don't treat me wrongly: I still want to please you,
    lad.
    What I've discovered leaves me in good heart.
  You won't get by me with deceit and tricks, you
    see:
    you've overtaken me and got the lead,
  but yet I'll stab you from behind, as once, they
    say,
    the daughter of Iasius, Atalanta,*

  For all her beauty she refused the love of men,
    girt herself up and ran—but all in vain.
  The gold-haired Atalanta left her father's house
    and disappeared into the mountain heights
  avoiding marriage, Aphrodite's lovely boon.—
    She learned at last, refuse it as she might.

1295-8 Don't get me all stirred up, lad, with my woes,
    or let my love for you bear me away
  down to Persephone's abode. Beware
    God's anger and men's gossip, and be kind.

1299-1304 How long, lad, will you run away? I'm chasing
    you,
    seeking you: let me have some finish-line

to catch you at! But you with proud and reckless
   heart
flee, with the cruel nature of a kite.
No, wait for me—give me your favour! Not for
   long
will blue-wreathed Aphrodite's boon be yours.

1305–10 The lovely bloom of boyhood's faster than a sprint
   in passing: ponder that, and let me off
the chain, or one day you too, cruel lad, may be
   oppressed and find the going hard in love,
as I do now towards you. Bear these points in
   mind,
   and don't succumb to bad . . .

1311–18 I saw you cheating on me, lad—I'm keeping track
   with these men that you're now in harmony
and friendship with, discarding my regard for you
   as worthless. You were not their friend before;
I thought to make of you my faithful comrade, you
   alone. Well, fine, now take another friend,
but I am down, your benefactor. Let no man,
   observing you, feel drawn to love of lads.

1319–22 Lad, as the Cyprian's made you so desirable
   and all the young men dote upon your looks,
hear what I say, and set your heart to favour me:
   accept that love's hard for a man to bear.

1323–6 Goddess of Cyprus, end my pain, disperse the
   cares
that gnaw my heart, restore my happiness,
break off my morbid brooding, grant me
   cheerfulness
   and better sense: I've had my span of youth.

1327–34 Lad, while your chin stays whiskerless, I'll never
   cease
praising you, even till my fated death.
It's graceful still for you to give, and no disgrace
   for me to ask. So, for our parents' sake,
show me respect, lad, and your favour: so may
   you
   in turn enjoy fair Aphrodite's boon

when you're in need and chase another lad. God
     grant
you get the same response that you give me!

1335-6   Happy the lover who can exercise at home—
in bed beside a nice lad, all day long.

1337-40 I love the lad no more: I've given pain the boot,
escaped from all that hassle with relief.
I stand released from fair-crowned Aphrodite's
     chains
of longing—but no thanks to you, my lad.

1351-2   Take an old man's advice: don't go carousing, lad.
For a young chap it isn't suitable.

1357-60 Lad-lovers always wear a stern yoke on their
     necks,
a harsh memento of convivial nights.
In working on a lad's affection, you've to set
your hand to a short-flaring vine-twig fire.

1361-2   You've lost my love, lad, run yourself upon a reef
and grabbed for safety at a rotten rope.

1363-4   I'll never harm you, even when we part. No man
will ever talk me out of loving you.

1365-6   Most handsome and adorable of lads,
stand there, just let me say a word or two.

1367-8   A lad shows gratitude, whereas a woman keeps
no lasting friend—she loves whoever's by.

1369-72 A lad's love's good to have, and good to lay aside,
much easier to find than to fulfil.
It comes with countless woes attached, and
     countless joys;
yet there's some pleasure even in the pain.

1373-4   You've never ever stayed for my sake. In response
to every earnest message, off you go.

1375-6   Happy lad-lover, if he's never known the sea
and does not fear benighting on the waves.

1377-80 Lad, you're a fine chap, but because of feckless
     friends
you mix with knaves and so disgrace yourself.

I didn't want to lose your friendship, but I'm glad
        I did, behaving as a free man should.

1381–5   We all thought you'd been sent to bring us
                something nice
            from golden Aphrodite . . .
            . . . but blue-wreathed Aphrodite's gift
        becomes a thing most burdensome for men to
                bear,
            unless the goddess grants deliverance.

1386–9   Goddess from Cyprus, cunning schemer, why did
                Zeus
            honour you with this special privilege?
        For you can overpower men's reason; there is none
            clever or strong enough to get away.

XENOPHANES

1   For now the floor is clean, and everybody's hands
        and cups; a servant garlands us with wreaths;
    another offers fragrant perfume from a dish;
        the mixing-bowl's set up, brimful of cheer,
    and further jars of wine stand ready, promising
        never to fail—soft wine that smells of flowers.
    The frankincense sends out its holy scent all round
        the room; there's water, cool and clear and
          sweet;
    bread lies to hand, gold-brown; a splendid table,
        too,
        with cheeses and thick honey loaded down.
    The altar in the middle's decked about with
        flowers;
        festivity and song pervade the house.
    The first thing men of sense should do is sing of
        God
        in words of holiness and purity,
    with a libation and a prayer for means to do
        what's right; that's more straightforward, after
          all,
    than crimes. Then drink what you can hold and
        still get home
        unaided (if, of course, you're not too old).
    Applaud the man who brings out good things in
        his cups,
        so that attention is attuned to good:
    don't be relating wars of Titans or of Giants
        or Centaurs, fictions of the men of old,
    or strife and violence. There's no benefit in that.
        No, always keep the gods duly in mind.

2   But if at running someone won a victory
        or in pentathlon* at Olympia
    by Pises' stream and Zeus's precinct, or again
        in wrestling, or the boxer's painful art,

or that demanding trial they call *pankration*,*
   he'd be more glamorous in the city's eyes;
he'd get a front seat at competitive events,
   and meals provided from the public purse
by vote of the city, and a prize to keep for aye—
   e'en if he won with steeds. He'd get all that
without deserving it as I do, for my brain
   is worth much more than men's or horses'
      brawn.
This custom's quite irrational; it isn't right
   to value brawn above the boon of brain.
For just because there's some good boxer in the
      town
   or some good wrestler or pentathlon man
or champion runner—which is most admired of all
   physical feats wherein men do compete—
that won't improve the law and order in the town;
   there's little joy for the community
in someone winning contests by the Pises' banks:
   that doesn't make the city's coffers fat.

3   And learning useless luxury from Lydia,
         while they were free from hateful tyranny,
       they'd go to the piazza in full purple robes,
         a thousand of them at the very least,
       proud in the splendour of their finely coiffured
          hair
         and sleek with unguents of the choicest scent.

5   Nor would one pour wine first to mix within the
         cup,
         but water first and wine on top of it.

6   You sent the thighbone of a kid, and got instead
         a fatted ox's leg—a worthy share
       for one whose fame will spread all over Greece,
         and last
         as long as there are singers in the land.

7–7a   Now I will start upon another argument
         and show the path . . . .

*(On Pythagoras)**

And once, they say, while he was passing by, he
    saw
  a puppy being beaten, and he said
'Oh, stop, don't thrash him—that's the soul of my
    good friend;
  I recognized it when I heard it yelp.'

8   Already threescore years and seven have passed
        away,
    batting my careworn consciousness through
        Greece,
  and there were five and twenty from my birth to
    then,
    if I can claim to know the truth of it.

9   Much feebler than a man advanced in age.

A 14   This is not an equal challenge, sinner versus moral
    man.

14   Yet mortal men imagine gods are born
  and dress like them, are shaped like them, and
    have their speech.

45   I batted myself on from town to town.

SIMONIDES

Victory Odes

506   Which of the men of today has bound on his
          brows
       in myrtle leaves or wreaths of rose
       so many victories in regional competition?

507   That Ram was duly fleeced*
       when he went to the splendid wooded precinct of
          Zeus.

508   As when in the month of storms
       Zeus chastens fourteen days,
       that men on earth call time of forgotten winds,
       holy brood-time of the coloured kingfisher.

509   Not even the strong Polydeuces
       would hold up his fists against him,
       or the iron son of Alcmena.*

511   [Heaven-bor]n Kronos' glorious son [himself]
       [honour]s Aiatios' clan; far-shooting
       Apollo of the golden lyre marks it out,
       and shining Delphi, where the horse-race . . .

           .   .   .   .   .   .

       [by proclamation most w]elcome
       they declared the man of Pyrrhus' line*
       king supreme of the province; and . . .
       with good fortune for Thessaly, and for all the
          people . . .

512   Drink, drink at this fortune!

515   Hail, daughters of storm-swift mares.*

516   And the dust went up from your chariot-wheel
       for the wind to carry away.

517   in case he let the brown straps slip from his hands.

519 fr. 79

>Whoever . . .
>let him be cheerful even though
>he's let . . . fall to the ground.
>Many men pray . . . and to win prestige
>by mounting fair-named Victory's car,
>but only for one does the goddess
>make room so he can leap
>aboard her great chariot.

519 fr. 92

>And may he walk round
>   . . . with a new race completed . . .
>   . . . cheerful . . . prosperity to come . . .
>   I rejoice, and hold a protecting arm
>about him, like a mother round her youngest son.

Paeans

519 fr. 32

>. . . of the doughty Carians . . .
>. . . on the banks of . . .'s streams they set up
>a fair [dance in the] meadows; for now [the
>   goddess]*
>was burdened with the private toils of birth.
>. . . cried out . . . from her holy womb, and . . .
>sent forth . . . Hear me . . .

519 fr. 35

>. . . from holy Parnes . . .
>. . . look dow]n, Apollo
>on the land of . . . Athena.
>. . . here well-disposed
>. . . spring will not pass.
>. . . we support the toil . . .
>. . . the virgin Artemis who runs
>in the mountains; and thee, far-shooting lord,
>we [hymn] with gentle [strains], uttering
>   auspicious cry
>that comes from hearts in concord.

519 fr. 55

> . . . the glens . . . Lycian [Apollo,]
> her finest of sons. Ië, ië!
> Cry hallelujah, Delian maids,
> with reverent [dance!]
>
> . . . .
>
> [when sp]ring comes. Lady of D[elos, gold of] face,
> . . . we in song . . . fortune . . .

519 fr. 77

> . . . of spring . . .
> . . . of white . . . garlands . . .
> . . . sprouting many a . . .
> and carrying many leaves
> of the native [bay?] he approached,
> regardless of Poseidon, the master of the earth.

Dirges

520
> Man's strength is but little, and futile his concerns,
> his lifespan short, filled with trouble on trouble;
> and over it death, inescapable, uniform, looms,
> to be dispensed in equal shares
> to high and low alike.

521
> As you are mortal, don't ever affirm what
>   tomorrow will bring,
> or how long the man that you see in good fortune
>   will keep it:
> not even the wing-spreading house-fly
> changes perch so fast.

522
> For all things come to the same
> Charybdis and are flushed away,
> all great distinction and wealth.

523
> Not even those of former times,
> hero sons of the lords of heaven,
> lived lives free of toil and danger and death
> unto old age.

524
> But then death overtakes
> even the man who flees from the fight.

526   None wins distinction without the gods, no man,
      no city. God is the one
      who can contrive all things: in mortal life
      nothing is safe from harm.

527   There is no ill that men should not expect;
      in a short space of time God
      reshuffles everything.

531   When men die [for their country,]
      fame is their fortune, fair their fate,
      their tomb an altar; in the place of wailing
      there is remembrance, and their dirge is praise.
      This winding-sheet is such
      as neither mould nor Time that conquers all
      can fade; this sepulchre
      of fine men has adopted as its sacristan
      Greece's good name. Witness Leonidas,*
      the king of Sparta: he has left
      a monument of valour, and perennial fame.

From various lyric poems

538   All larks must sport a crest.

541   . . . distinguishes fair and foul. And if
      someone who has no shutters to his mouth
      cavils, why, smoke is ineffectual stuff,
      gold does not stain, and truth
      alone prevails. But God
      grants few men such distinction as endures
      throughout: it is no easy thing
      to keep high standards, for despite himself
      a man is overborne
      by irresistible desire of gain
      or the scheming Love-goddess's compelling itch
      or lively rivalries.
      Still, if he cannot keep
      the path of sanctity throughout his life,
      but to his best ability . . .

542   For a man to be truly good is difficult,
      fashioned foursquare in hands and feet and mind
      without a blemish . . .

Nor does the saying of Pittacus ring true
to me, although a wise man was its source:
he said that being good was *difficult*.
That honour's God's alone: a man
can't help but sink, if he be caught
by helpless circumstance.
Any man's good if his affairs go well,
and bad if they go badly; so
they're best for longest, whom the immortals bless.

Therefore I will not waste my allotted span
of life in vain and insubstantial hope,
trying to find what is not possible,
a perfect human soul, of all
of us who cull the broad earth's fruits—
I'll tell you if I do.
No, I commend and favour anyone
who does no scurvy thing from choice—
even the gods can't fight necessity.

. . . I'm not bent
on finding fault. It's good enough for me
if someone's not a rogue or too
shiftless, and knows the public good
that comes from righteousness,
a sane man; I'll not criticize him, for
the breed of fools is infinite.
All things are fair that have no foul mixed in.

543   . . . Danae, when in the carven chest*
the wind blowing and the sea stirring
shattered her with fear. Her cheeks were wet
as she put her loving arm round Perseus, saying,
'Oh, child! What trouble is mine,

yet you can slumber, in your innocence
snoring on comfortless timber, bronze-riveted,
in the black gloom of unlit night.
The passing wave's deep spray upon your hair
disturbs you not, or the wind's keening,
as you lie in your royal-red shawl, bonny face.

If fear were fear to you,
even the sound of my words
would catch your tiny ear.

Yes, sleep, baby; and sleep, sea!
Sleep, measureless misery!
O father Zeus,
grant some sign of a change of thy will;
and if I speak too bold at all, or out of place,
forgive me.'

571   and I am paralysed
       by the din of the purple brine as it surges all
               round.

545 (Jason)
       He settled in Corinth, he did not dwell
       in Magnesia; and living with his Colchian wife
       he ruled over Thranos and Lechaeum.

550 (Aegeus gave Theseus)
       a red sail, stained with the juice
       of the springing holm-oak's bloom.

551   I would have brought you a greater blessing—life—
       had I come earlier.*

553   They wept for violet-wreathed Eurydice's
       poor unweaned babe, as he
       breathed out his sweet life-soul.

555   well given by Hermes god of the contest, son
       of Maia, the mountain nymph with curling lashes,
       loveliest of the seven
       dear dark-tressed daughters that Atlas fathered,
               called
       the Doves of heaven, the Peleiades.*

559   As for you, mother of twenty,
       be gracious, Hecuba.

564   . . . Meleager, who in the javelin
       beat all the young men, hurling
       over Anauros' eddying stream
       from Iolcus' vineland: so have Homer
       and Stesichorus sung the tale to all.

595   For not so much as a breeze to shake a leaf
       then moved, that might prevent
       the honeysweet voice of the Sirens as it spread abroad
       from lodging in their mortal ears.*

567   And over Orpheus' head
       birds without number flew,
       while straight up from the darkling wave
       the fish leapt to his lovely song.

572   Against the men of Corinth
       Ilios nurses no wrath, nor the Danaans.

575 (Eros)
       You cruel child of scheming Aphrodite
       that she bore to the evil god of war.

577(a) (Cassotis,*)
       where for cleansing of hands
       the lovely-haired Muses' holy water is drawn
           from below.

577(b)   Clio, that watchest over the holy
       cleansing of hands . . . gold-robed . . .
       as for many a prayer they draw
       the lovely, fragrant water from the ambrosial
           depths.

579   There is a tale
       that Merit dwells on high rocks, hard to climb
       . . . patrols the holy place.
       Not all men's eyes may look upon her—only he
       who sheds heart-stinging sweat
       and reaches the summit of manly endeavour.

581   Who of sound mind could assent
       to that Lindian, Cleobulus,* who against
       the perennial flow of rivers, the flowers of spring,
       the flame of the sun, the gold of the moon
       and swirl of the sea
       pitted the strength of a mere *tombstone*?
       All things yield to the gods: a stone
       even man's arts can shatter. That was the thought
           of a fool.

582   Even silence has its reward of safety.

583   You cock of delightful voice.

584   For, void of pleasure, what human life's
           desirable, what monarchy?
           Without that, even the gods' eternity
           were nothing enviable.

585   From her red mouth
           the girl gave voice.

586   When the twittering
           sallow-necked nightingales of spring . . .

587   For this was what the Centaurs most abhorred:
               fi-ire.*

590   Even what's tough
           becomes attractive in emergencies.

591   Horse-breeding does not go
           with a Zacynthus, but with fertile acres.

592   Beside the pure refiner's gold
           not even having lead to show.

593   The bee frequents the flowers,
           contriving the yellow honey.

594   A glorious reputation
           is the last thing to sink below the earth.

597   Sonorous harbinger of fragrant spring,
           blue swallow.

598   Appearance even overbears the truth.

599   And he with sweet sleep in his gift . . .

600   A wind pricking into the sea.

601   Man-mastering sleep.

602   The new wine cannot yet
           discredit last year's offering from the vine.
           This is the empty-headed claim of boys.*

603   For what has come to pass
           will not now be undone.

604   Not even lovely skill in poetry
           gives any joy, unless one has
           the dignity of health.

605   There's only one sun in the sky.

Elegiac poems

The Battle of Artemisium

el. 3   by the immortals' will . . . .
      Zetes and Kalaïs* . . .

         .   .   .   .   .

         .   .   .   .

         .   .   .

[They came as swif]t as dee[r, the sons of Boreas]
   [and Oreithyia,] maid with lovely hair.
[They stirred the] sea up from its murky bed, [and
      roused]
   [the Old Man, b]right-famed [guardian] of the
      deep,
[who spoke in prophecy:] 'What is this distant
      [din]
   [I hear] b[rush]ing my ears, [as of a battle?']

el. 9   throwing sticks and stones upon . . .

The Battle of Plataea

el. 10   . . . for m[y compos]ition . . .
      [O son of] sea-[nymph],* glorious in thy fame.

el. 11   str[uck you . . . and you fell, as when a larch]
      or pine-tree in the [lonely mountain] glades
is felled by woodcutters . . .
      and much . . .
[A great grief seized] the war-host; [much they
      honoured you,]
   [and with Patr]oclus' [ashes mingled yours.]
[It was no ordinary mortal] laid you low,
   ['twas by Apoll]o's hand [that you were struck.]
[Athena] was at [hand, and smote the famous
      t]ow[n]
   [with Hera: they were wro]th with Priam's sons
[because of P]aris' wickedness. The car of God's
   Justice o'ertakes [the sinner in the end.]
[And so] the valiant Danaans, [best of warr]iors,
   sacked the much-sung-of city, and came [home;]

[and they] are bathed in fame that cannot die, by
    grace
 [of one who from the dark-]tressed Muses had
the tru[th entire,] and made the heroes'
    short-lived race
 a theme familiar to younger men.
[But] now farewell, [thou son] of goddess glorious,
    [daughter] of Nereus of the sea, while I
[now summon] thee, i[llustriou]s Muse, to my
    support,
 [if thou hast any thought] for men who pray:
[fit ou]t, as is thy wont, this [grat]eful song-a[rray]
  [of mi]ne, so that rem[embrance is preserved]
of those who held the line for Spart[a and for
    Greece,]
 [that none should see] the da[y of slavery.]
They kept their co[urage, and their fame rose]
    heaven-high;
 [their glory in] the world [will] never die.
[From the Eu]rotas and from [Sparta's] town they
    [marched,]
  accompanied by Zeus' horsemaster sons,
[the Tyndarid] Heroes, and by Menelaus'
    strength,*
 [those doughty] captains of [their fath]ers' folk,
led forth by [great Cleo]mbrotus' most noble [son,]
    . . . . Pausanias.
[They quickly reached the Isthmus] and the
    famous land
  of Corinth, [furthest bounds] of Pelops' [isle,]
[and Megara, N]isus' [ancient] city, where the
    r[est]
  [then joined the army from] the country round.
[Again they marched, the ome]ns giving
    confidence,
  [and soon they reached Eleusis'] lovely plain,
driving [the Persians from Pan]dion's [land, by
    help]
  of that most godlike se[er, the Iamid.*]
. . . overcame . . .

el. 13   to drive away [the army] of the Medes
and Persians, and . . .
            the sons of Dorus* and of Heracles.
        When they [came down] into [the broad Boeotian]
                plain
            and [the Medes] facing them came into view,
        . . . they sat down (?) . . .

el. 14 (*Prophecy of Tisamenus*)
            [. . . cl]ash of blows on [shields]
            [. . . I de]clare that, should the a[rmy pr]ess
                [across] the river* first . . .
        a great disaster will [be theirs; but if they wait,]
            [a victory that] ne'er shall be for[got.]
        [And . . .] will drive them [out of A]si[a too]
            [with Zeus'] approval, favouring a n[ew]
        alliance; for [. . . will la]y a firm base . . .

el. 15+16
        And in the centre stood well-watered Ephyra's
                men,
            well versed in every martial excellence,
        and those who dwelt in Corinth, Glaucus' capital.
            They had the finest witness to their work—
        of precious gold, in heaven, one that magnifies
            their fathers' far-famed glory with their own.

el. 19   This finest single thing the Chian said:*
        'As is the breed of leaves, e'en so is that of man.'
            Few mortals who have had that in their ears
        have taken it to heart, for everyone relies
            on hope; it's planted in a young man's breast.

el. 20   . . . only a short time . . .
            . . . abiding . . .
        A mortal, while he has the lovely bloom of youth,
            has many empty-headed, vain ideas.
        He has no expectation of old age or death,
            and while in health, has no thought of disease.
        They're fools who have that attitude, and do not
                know
            the time allowed to us for youth and life

is short. Take note of this, and till your days are
        done
    don't waver, treat your soul to all that's nice.
. . . Ponder the [saying of a man] of old—
    for Homer's tongue's escaped [oblivion;]
all-conquer[ing Time has spared him, never
        dimmed his name,]
    [and never found his testimony] false.
. . . in festivity . . .
    . . . well-turned [arguments (?)]

el. 21   My soul, I cannot be your watchful guardian.
            I've ruefully respected pure-faced Right
        ever since first I saw on my young growing thighs
            the signs that my boy's life was at an end,
        and that the ivory gleam was interspersed with
                black,
            and from the snows . . .
        Restrained by in[hibition . . .] youth's disorderly
            . . .

el. 22   I should like to sail
            [with cargo] of the dark-wreathed [Muses'] art
        and come to that tree-shaded home [of sainted
                men,]
            that airy island where life has its crown;
        and there I'd see my auburn Echecratidas
            [with these old ey]es, and take him by the hand,
        so that his lovely skin's young bloom [should
                breathe on me,]
            and he'd distil sweet longing from his eyes.
        Reclining [with the l]ad among the flowers, I'd
                [have]
            [a lovely time, slough] my white wrinkles off;
        and for my hair I'd weave a fresh, delightful
                wreath
            of new-sprung [galingale . . .]
        and I would sing a charming, clear-voiced [song of
                love,]
            plying my tongue in elo[quent . . .]

el. 23   Wine, defence against unhappiness.

el. 24   Nothing of Bacchus' must be cast aside,
          even a grape-pip.

el. 25   The stuff* with which the North Wind, rushing
              down from Thrace,
              once made a covering for Olympus' flanks,
          and stung the hearts of cloakless men, and then
              withdrew,
              buried alive in the Pierian soil—
          let me be served my share of that too. It's not nice
              to bring a friend a warm drink for a toast.

el. 26   For broad as it was,* it did not reach to me.

el. 86   But if, daughter of Zeus, the best must be
              acclaimed,
              then Athens' people did it all alone.

el. 87   And best of witnesses, the gold that shines in
              heaven.

el. 88   Time has sharp teeth, and gnaws
          all things away, even the mightiest.

el. 89   For memory none, I claim, can match Simonides,
          eighty years old, son of Leoprepes.

el. 90   A man learns from the community.

el. 91   When I behold the tomb of Megacles,
          I feel your suffering, poor Callias.

el. 92*   Muse, sing to me of the fair-ankled Alcmena's son:
          the son of Alcmena sing to me, Muse, the
              fair-ankled one.

SUSARION

Oyez, Oyez! Announcement by Susarion,
Philinus' son, Megarian from Tripodisc.
Woman's a pest. But all the same, parishioners,
no household can exist without aforesaid pest:
for marry or stay single, either's damnable.

APOLLODORUS

Who at such a time
has come to the edge of the doorway?

CYDIAS

714   Mind you don't become
                a fawn in the face of a lion
                seeking a share of the meat.

948   A far-faring call of the lyre.

PRATINAS

708   What commotion is this?* What cavortings are
        these?
    What hooliganism's invading the old Dionysiac
        knockabout altar?
    He's mine, my Bromios, mine is the clamour, the
        banging,
    the speeding over the mountains with the Naiads,
    shaping a dapple-winged melody like a swan.
    The Muse established singing as queen: let the
        pipe,
    being the servant, dance in second place,
    content to take the field
    only for drunken young fellows' carousing and
        brawling on doorsteps.
    Smash the burbling windy toad,
    burn the spit-wasting-reedy, the
        deep-voiced-chattering,
    the out-of-tune/rhythm-step creature of
        drill-moulded body.
    Here, look here! This is the way
    to fling your right arm and your leg!
    Thriambus-dithyrambus, lord with ivy crown,
    give ear, give ear to this my Dorian dance!

709   The chirper's a Laconian, well set for the dance.

710   Not ploughing furrowed land
    but seeking virgin soil.

711   sweet-voiced quail.

712   Do not pursue either the tense
    or the relaxed Ionian Muse,*
    but plough the intermediate field
    and be Aeolian in your song . . .
    . . . Befitting
    all song-roisterers
    is the Aeolian tuning.

ANONYMOUS PARTY SONGS

884   Pallas Tritogeneia, queen Athena,
keep this town on its feet, and all its people,
   so it's free from griefs, free from disputes,
free from untimely deaths—you and your father Zeus.

885   Of Demeter, of Wealth's Olympian mother,
let me sing at this time of wearing garlands,
   and of thee, O Persephone, Zeus'
daughter: both hail, and take care of this city well.

886   Once in Delos did Leto bear her children,
Phoebus golden of hair, the lord Apollo,
   and the one who shoots deer in the wild,
Artemis, who for all women has power supreme.

887   O Pan, ruler of far-renowned Arcadia,
dance-companion of nymphs of Dionysus:
   may you smile, O Pan, favourably,
gratified by this glad-spirited song of mine.

888   We're victorious as we hoped we would be:
the gods gave us the victory; they brought it
   from Pandrosos . . .
. . . beloved Athena . . .

889   Oh, if only one could examine each man's
nature, open his chest to check his feelings;
   then you'd close it back up again, then
truly acknowledge him friend with an open heart.

890   Health's the finest of all things for a mortal;
second-best is to be attractive-looking;
   and the third-best's wealth, honest-john wealth;
fourth-best's enjoying life's prime with your
      favourite pals.

892   Now this is what the crab said
as the snake in his claw he caught:
   'A friend should be straightforward,
and think no devious thought.'

893   I will carry my sword in sprigs of myrtle
       like Harmodius and Aristogeiton*
           when they killed the foul tyrant, and made
       Athens a place of laws equal for everyone.

894   Dear Harmodius, you're not dead, I'm sure:
       in the Isles of the Blest, they say, you're settled,
           where Achilles fleet-footed is too,
       and, as they say, the good Diomede, Tydeus' son.

895   I will carry my sword in sprigs of myrtle
       like Harmodius and Aristogeiton
           on Athena's great festival day,
       when they both struck the foul tyrant Hipparchus
           dead.

896   Your great glory will live on earth for ever,
       dear Harmodius and Aristogeiton,
           that you killed the foul tyrant, and made
       Athens a place of laws equal for everyone.

898   Son of Telamon, spearman Ajax, you, they say,
       were best of the Danaans, after Achilles, that went
           to Troy.

899   Telamon was the first, they say, and Ajax next
       of the Danaans, after Achilles, that went to Troy.

900   I wish I were a lovely lyre of ivory,
       and lovely boys would take me to
       their dithyrambic dance.

901   I wish I were a lovely pendant, big, fine gold,
       and a lovely lady would wear me
       with purity in her heart.

902   Drink with me, frolic and love with me, with me
           put on the garland;
       rave with me when I rave, and when I'm sober, be
           sober.

904   The old sow's got a nice acorn,
           but has her heart set on another;
       and I've got one pretty girl,
           but have my heart set on another.

905   Bath-attendants and tarts
       practise parallel arts:
       they douse tramp and toff
       in one communal trough.

907   Oh, Leipsydrion,* that betrayed our comrades,
       oh, what men you've destroyed, both good in
            battle
         and of noble blood, men who indeed
       showed on that day from what fathers they had
            their birth.

908   He who betrays not his friend wins great esteem
       among both mortals and gods, as I opine.

909   I'm plenty rich, I've got my spear, my sword,
       my lovely oxhide to protect my skin.
         With this I sow, with this I reap,
       with this I tread the sweet wine from the grapes,
       with this I'm titled master of the serfs.

       And those not bold enough for spear, for sword,
       for lovely oxhide to protect their skins,
         why, they all cower at my knees,
       prostrate themselves . . .
       addressing me as master and great king.

911   Never ever was such a man in Athens
       as Harmodius and Aristogeiton.

912(a) You cannot play the fox
       or be friends with both sides.

912(b) Money and livelihood
       for me and Clitagora
       with the Thessalians.

913   A mortal man needs little—only love
       and fodder; but you're really miserly.

Both attendants and ...
practise parallel arts
they dance tramp and toil
in one communal trough.

Oh, Leipsydrion, that betrayed our comrades,
oh, what men you've destroyed, both good in battle
and of noble blood, men who indeed
showed on that day from what fathers they and
their birth.

He who betrays not his friend wins great esteem
among both mortals and gods, as honour.

I'm plenty rich, I've got my spear, my sword,
my lovely oxhide to protect my skin.
With this I sow, with this I reap,
with this I tread the sweet wine from the grapes
with this I'm titled master of the serfs.

And those not bold enough for spear, for sword,
for lovely oxhide to protect their skins,
why, they all cower at my knees,
prostrate themselves,
addressing me as master and great king.

Never ever was such a man in Athens
as Harmodius and Aristogeiton.

You cannot play the fox,
or be friends with both sides.

Money and livelihood
for me and Chiragora
with the Thessalians.

A mortal man needs little—only love
and fodder; but you're ready already.

Fifth Century

TELESILLA

717 **Here is Artemis, maidens,
fleeing from Alpheus.***

TIMOCREON

727*   Well, you may approve of Pausanias or of
          Xanthippus
    or Leotychidas, but I approve
    of Aristides as the one best man
    to come from Athens, since Themistocles
    forfeits the favour of Leto:

    the criminal liar and traitor, who, bribed by the
          silver
    of knaves, refused to help Timocreon
    his friend back to his home, Ialysos,
    but took three silver talents and sailed off
    into the sunset, to blazes,

    restoring some wrongfully, killing or exiling others;
    and at the Isthmus,* loaded up to here
    with cash, he made a comical Mine Host
    and served the meat cold. So they ate, and prayed
    God for Themistocles' ruin.

728   Muse, make this song famous through Greece,
    as is only right and proper.

729*   Oho, Timocreon
    is not the only one
    to come to terms with Medes!
    No, there are other knaves,
    I'm not the only fox,
    there's other Reynards too!

731   Blind god of wealth, you never ought
    to have appeared on land or sea
    or anywhere: you ought to stay
    in Tartarus, by Acheron,
    for all men's ills are due to you.

732   A smart Sicilian
    said to his mum . . .

Iambic and elegiac fragments

7   Once, long ago, Milesians were brave.

9   His brain's there to advise, but not his hand.

10   Some Cean blather* fell on my reluctant ears:
     on my reluctant lugs some blather fell from Ceos.

EUENUS

<table>
<tr><td>1</td><td>

Many men tend to contradict on every point,
    but contradicting *rightly*'s out of vogue.
Well, as for them there's one old saw that's all we
      need:
    'you can keep your opinion, I'll keep mine.'
But the intelligent are soon persuadable
    by reason, and they're easiest to teach.
</td></tr>
<tr><td>2</td><td>

Bacchus is measured best not too much, nor too
      small—
    that causes either gloom or mania.
He likes to make a foursome with three
      water-nymphs:*
    that's when he's best equipped for bedding up,
for if he blows too strong, he turns desire away,
    and plunges you in sleep—next thing to death.
</td></tr>
<tr><td>3</td><td>

I hold that not the smallest part of being wise
    is knowing truly what each man is like.
</td></tr>
<tr><td>4</td><td>

Resolve combined with wisdom brings much
      benefit;
    without it, it brings harm and misery.
</td></tr>
<tr><td>5</td><td>

Often men's anger will lay bare their hidden mind;
    insanity is nowhere near so bad.
</td></tr>
<tr><td>6</td><td>

A son means either fear or pain full-time.
</td></tr>
<tr><td>7</td><td>

                        Contumely,
which brings no gain and none the less does wrong.
</td></tr>
<tr><td>8a</td><td>

Detain not any of these guests against his will,
    nor urge departure if he wants to stay;
don't wake him up, Simonides, if one of us,
    well laced with wine, falls prey to gentle sleep,
and don't insist he sleep, if he is wide awake:
    compulsion's always disagreeable.
If someone wants to drink, let slaves stand by to pour;
    one doesn't get a nice time every night.
</td></tr>
</table>

But I'll go home—I've had my measure of sweet
    wine—
  and think of sleep, that frees us from all ills.
I've reached the stage where wine sits sweetest in
    a man:
  I'm neither sober, nor unduly drunk.
When someone overshoots the measure of his
    drink,
  he's no more in control of tongue and mind.
He says wild things that make the sober blush, and
    feels
  no shame in anything he does while drunk—
a level-headed man before, but now a fool.
  Take note of this, and do not drink too much,
but either rise before you're drunk (don't let your
    greed
  bully you like some wretched daily help)
or, if you stay, don't drink. But no, you always
    chirp
  this foolish 'Fill her up!' That's why you're
    drunk.
Yes, one's a loving-cup, another's been set up,
  one's for the gods' libation, one's a sconce—
you can't say no. In truth, your champion's he that
    drinks
  cup after cup and yet says nothing rude.
Well, stay and make good talk beside your
    mixing-bowl;
  avoid disputes as long as e'er you may;
speak openly, let all hear what you say to one:
  that way a party turns out not half bad.

8b   If I had wealth, Simonides, as once I had,
    I'd not feel bad in high-class company;
  but now I see it pass me by, and I've no voice,
    from want, though I'd have judged better than
      most
  that we're adrift, our white sails shipped before the
    storm,
    upon the Melian sea* in blackest night.

They can't agree to bale out, while the waves wash
    in
  on both sides. We can scarce hope to survive,
the way they're going on: they've sacked the
    excellent
  helmsman who always kept such skilful watch;
they're plundering the cargo, and all order's gone;
  there's no more sharing out on equal terms;
the porters rule; rogues lord it over men of worth.
I fear the sea may swallow up the ship.
There, that's my coded message to the upper class;
  and even a hick may grasp it, if he's smart.

8c Alas, I love a soft-skinned lad, who shows me up
      to all our friends against my every wish.
    I'll bear it unconcealed—one's often forced to
        things;
      it's no bad-looking boy I've fallen for.
    Boy-love's a pleasure; after all, once Kronos' son,
        king of immortals, fell for Ganymede,
    seized him and took him to Olympus, gave him
        rank
      divine, with all his lovely boyhood's bloom.
    Therefore, Simonides, don't wonder if I too
      am found in thrall to a delightful lad.

9   I hold it is long practice, friend, and this
    constitutes human nature in the end.

10 The cleverest and most stupid thing is—time.

LAMPROCLES

735   Pallas the sacker of cities I hymn, the valiant virgin
horse-taming daughter of mighty Zeus.

736   Pleiades, you that are set in the sky
sharing the name of the doves that fly.

ATTRIBUTED TO TERPANDER

697   Once more of the lord far-shooting
            let my heart sing.

698   Zeus, thou first of all,
            that lead'st the way for all,
            O Zeus, I send to thee
            this first fruit of my songs.

PRAXILLA

747 (*Adonis' lament in the underworld*)

>The sun's light is the finest thing I leave behind,
>and next the shining stars and the moon's face,
>and the ripe apples, pears, and cucumbers.

748 (*Achilles*)

>But they could ne'er persuade the heart within
>   your breast.

749=897

>Mark the saying of Admetus, my friend: cleave to
>   the men of class,
>keep away from the rogues, seeing that rogues
>   seldom show gratitude.

750=903

>Let me warn you, my friend: scorpions lie hid
>   under every stone:
>watch out lest you get stung: what you can't see
>   bodes every sort of trap.

754

>O Miss, from out your window blowing kisses—
>a Miss by your face, but lower down a Mrs.

Anonymous Fragments
(Various Dates)

Iambic fragments

1   Plenty of space, by courtesy of Syloson.*

2   And many are the waves of the wide sea
the South Wind rolls between us.

3   Abdera, Teos' fair-built colony.

5   To Xanthe, aged lady, much beloved
by women.

36   Go on, tread on their necks, yes, tread them to the
ground.

37   A stout-legged woman grinding corn, being jigged
against the millstone.

39a   I am enfeebled, I have little strength.

50   Crying 'Bow wow!' and barking like a dog.

52   I'm in love, Leucippus, under a lucky nuthatch.

55   Either a treble six or a treble one.

55a   And this is what he said:
'Thine is the power, O king.'

56   He's gone off
taking the loot for himself.

Elegiac fragments

1   Sons of Ariston, godlike stock of famous sire.

2   Whereas a man of worth's now wretch, now gent.

2a   As wolves love a lamb, so lovers love a lad.

3   Goodness is one; of vice there's every sort.

4   Many a friendship by not speaking's been
dissolved.

5 Athenians no longer know Megarians.

6 Pour one for Kedon,* waiter, do not leave him out,
   if men of quality deserve their wine.

7 The South-West wind soon clouds, soon clears the
     sky,
   but the Northwester brings up all the clouds.

8 I care no more for music or for song.

9 This was the rightest of all his wrongful deeds.

10 He was a good man, but he met his better.

11 Girls lifting their light footsteps in the dance.

12 Even the worthless man's esteemed in times of
     strife.

13 At long last we have both come to our senses, lad.

17 Over the Stenyclerian Plain, to the mountain top,
   Aristomenes* pursued the Spartan foe.

19 The gods implanted no good sense in piper-men:
   even as they blow, their brains fly out as well.

20 And we sailed off into the Hellespont.

21 Zeus alone has cures for everything.

22 For any issue there's no better test than time,
   which brings even men's inmost thoughts to
     light.

23 If only hidden opportunity were plain
   to see. It's best increased by wariness.

24 Endure even a harsh deal from the gods.

25 Youth's always wayward; that's how human beings
     are.
   Far worse, though, if it injures what is right.

26 To the watchman his watch, to the lover his errand
   of love.

27 Hail, fellow drinkers, agemates: from this happy
     start
   I'll bring my discourse to a happy end.
   When friends foregather for occasions such as this,
   we ought to laugh and joke in high-class style,

    enjoy each other's company, make silly chat
      and banter such as fosters merriment.
The serious talk should follow, with each speaker
      heard
    in turn: that's what symposiums are for.
But let's be guided by the MC: that's what fine
    fellows must do, and show their eloquence.

Melic fragments

873   You lads who are blessed with charm and with fine
        fathers,
    do not begrudge society your bloom,
    for beside manliness
    relaxing Love too flourishes
    in Chalcis' townships.

878   He pipes on Mariandyne reeds,
    striking Ionian notes.

938(f)   O father Zeus, I wish I could be rich.

941   Now make we libation
    to Memory's daughters
    the Muses, and likewise
    the Muses' leader,
    the son of Leto.

942   Polyhymnia,* maid who gives delight to all.

943   More delicate than a narcissus.

944 (A woman speaks)
                      Do not wear out
    my own swift feet, or my brothers' (sisters'?).

946   The destiny of men
    who have won the highest rank
    goes on to its goal.

947   For the Muse does not shiftlessly
    taste only what's before her, but advances
    harvesting everything . . .
    Pray do not make her stop,
    now that delightful melodies have been started
    by the fair-crying pipe with its manifold notes.

950(*a*) God born in Delos, whether you are now in
      Lycia . . .

950(*b*) Golden-haired Archer, son of Zeus.

950(*c*) And then the earth
      and the world stream's waters vanished into
         night.

952   (*Zeus gave Alcmena a goblet*)
      And she took and admired straightway the golden
         cup.

955   Artemis, my heart desires
      to weave you a beautiful hymn,
      while another takes up in her hands
      the bronze-faced castanets that gleam like gold.

957   Asteris, neither I nor Apelles loves you.

961   Never will I accept prestige as the reward
      of dishonest gain.

964   Countless garlands decorate the earth.

975   If you oversee the rites
      of the white-armed goddess of love.

976   (*A woman sings*)
      The moon and the Pleiads have quit the sky;
         the small hours lie ahead.
      The time for love is passing by,
         and I'm alone in my bed.

978(*a*) And Zeus' high hall resounded.

978(*b*) Hearken, daughter of Zeus and . . .

986   The highest state of man
      is to enjoy what's fine, and have the means.

989   Ilion perished in flames over Helen.

998   (*Castor and Pollux aid sailors in storms,*)
      softening the violent sea's assault
      and the wind's swift blasts.

999   Stowing the great sail away at the foot of the mast
      he runs from the darkling sea.

1000   . . . before the storm, as at
      a sea-cape with the North Wind blowing sharp.

1001   I declare
       the dark-tressed Muses have dealt him well.

1002   I hate to drink with anyone
       inclined to remember things.

1004   When the seaman is struck by his want of the
           Tyndarid brothers.*

1005   Over the calm, clear-shining water
       with smiling face there came to them the longing
       for a bench in a ship to scar the sea,
       assaulting the divine.

1007   Not sand or dust or feathers of birds of varied
           plumage
       would pile up in such profusion.

1009   Then he will lie in the deep-wooded earth,
       excluded from symposiums, lyre-music,
       and the pipes' delightful cry.

1011   Going to see Helen of the curling lashes.

1014   But she, the cause of much strife,
       the lady Helen . . .

1016   Hymn we the Blessed Ones, Muses, Zeus'
           daughters,
       in songs that shall not perish.

1017 (*On Fate*)
       And what she approves with even a nod of her
           brows
       must submit to the dispensation
       of powerful necessity.

Work songs

849   Toss me the mostest sheaf, toss me a sheaf!

869   Grind, mill, grind:
       even Pittacus used to grind,
       the ruler of great Mytilene.

Play songs

852   Where are my roses, where are my violets,
  where's my pretty celery?
 Here are the roses, here are the violets,
  here's the pretty celery.

861*   I'm bringing out a lame little billy-goat.

875*   'Who's got the pot—' '—on the boil?'
 'Who's at the pot?' 'Me, Midas!'

876a *(Blind Man's Buff)**
 'I'll hunt this brazen fly.'
 'You'll hunt, but you won't catch!'

876(b) Shine, sun, we love you!*

876(c) 'Torty-tortoise,* what are you at in the middle?'
 'I'm winding wool, Milesian thread I twiddle.'
 'And that baby of yours, now how did he get
  himself bumped?'
 'Off the white horses into the sea he JUMPED!'

Ritual songs

848 The swallow, the swallow is here,*
  bringing a fine new year:
  white belly, dark back;
  so from your rich rack
  roll out a fruit-pack,
  a cup of wine, please,
  and a punnet of cheese;
  or a bran-loaf or pulse-loaf or so—
  the swallow won't say no.
  Do we go on our road,
  or get what we're owed?
 Give something, fine; if not, we won't let be,
 we'll take the door, or else the lintel-piece,
 or else the lady sitting there inside—
 she's not so big, we'll fetch her easily.
 So if you're bringing something, make it big.
 Open up to the swallow, open your door:
 it's only children knocking, not old men!

851(*a*)   Keep back, make way for the god:*
           erect and bursting, he wants to pass straight through.

854   Rain, dear Zeus, rain*
           on our ploughland and plain.

856   Come along now, all you sons*
           of manly Sparta's citizens.
           Left arm up to defend with shield,
           right arm bravely the spear to wield,
           with never a thought your life to save—
           that's not the old Spartan way to behave.

857   Come along now, sons of Sparta, in your armour
               to dance the war-god's dance.

862   A holy boy is born*
           to the lady Brimo: Brimos.

868   To Athens let us go.*

870   Young, valiant warriors we used to be.*
           —And we are now: inspect us if you will.
           —And we will be in time, far stronger yet!

871   Come to the festival, O Dionysus,*
           to the Eleans' holy temple,
           with the spirits of joy
           enter on bovine hoof,
           worthy bull! Worthy bull!

872   Put off our old age till later,*
           O lovely Aphrodite!

877   Pass by(?) the bridge, O Maiden;*
           more than ever's thrice ploughed.

879(1)*   Invoke the god.
           —Iacchus, Semele's son, giver of wealth!

879(2)   Who's by?—A crowd of worthy men!

879(3)   The wine is poured: invoke the god.

881(*b*)   Out you go,
           croaky crow!*

882   Take good fortune*
               and take good health
           that we bring from the goddess,
               that she called for herself.

EXPLANATORY NOTES

Archilochus

Epodes: the ancients gave this name to those poems of Archilochus that were in simple strophic form, with one or two short lines following a longer one. In some cases we can group enough fragments together from the same poem to get an idea of its overall plan.

20 *Magnesia's*: Magnesia on the Maeander was a Greek town in Asia Minor. Its sack by the Cimmerians (see the note on Callinus 5*a*) sent a shock-wave through Greece.

22 *the Siris river lands*: a site in south Italy that attracted colonists from Ionia.

105 *Glaucus, see*: the impending storm is metaphorical. According to the author who quotes the fragment, it stands for battle with Thracians. The heights of Gyrae were some 25 miles north of Paros. Fragment 106 may belong to the same poem.

19 *Gyges*: king of Lydia, the most powerful state in western Asia Minor. He reigned from about 687 to 652.

24 *Gortyn*: one of the principal towns of Crete at this period.

26 *destroy them as you do destroy*: the verb is *apollyō*, which Apollo's name naturally suggested to a Greek ear.

2 *Ismaros*: in Thrace, the source of a celebrated wine.

5 *Saian*: a Thracian tribe.

Semonides

6 *A wife?*: these two lines are a close paraphrase of Hesiod, *Works and Days* 702–3.

20 *Maia's son*: Hermes, a god of herdsmen.

Callinus

5*a* *Cimmerian horde*: the Cimmerians were a people from north of the Black Sea. In the late eighth century BC, displaced by Scythian invaders, a large number of them crossed the Caucasus, and over the next half-century they butted their way across Asia Minor, eventually reaching the Aegean.

Eumelus

696* From a processional composed for a Messenian men's chorus to sing at a festival on Delos. Ithome was a mountain in Messene; the god worshipped there was Zeus.

Tyrtaeus

2 *Pelops' broad sea-circled land*: the Peloponnese. Tyrtaeus refers to the legendary migration of the Dorians from central Greece in alliance with Heracles' son Hyllus, whose grandsons or great-grandsons established the three Peloponnesian kingdoms of Sparta, Argos, and Messene.

19 *Pamphyloi, Hylleis, and Dymanes*: the three traditional Dorian tribes, one supposedly descended from Hyllus, the other two from sons of Aegimius, who was a son of Dorus, the mythical ancestor of the Dorians.

23a *the Aegis*: an impenetrable goatskin that guarantees victory; in Homer it is held by Zeus or Athena. Hence our expression 'under the aegis of —'.

Mimnermus

4 *Tithonus*: the mythical Trojan whose beauty so appealed to the Dawn-goddess that she carried him off for herself. She begged Zeus to grant him everlasting life, which he did; but she had not thought to specify everlasting *youth*, so he just gets older and older and older.

9 *Aipy we left*: a town in Messene. Mimnermus refers to the legend of an early migration from Messene to Asia Minor.

11 *that great fleece*: the Golden Fleece that the Argonauts journeyed to a distant eastern land to get. This was a task laid upon Jason by Pelias, king of Iolcus.

12 *Aethiopia*: the land of the mythical Aethiopes, who dwell close to the sunrise. Only later was the name settled on the people of Sudan.

14 *Hermos*: a river north of Smyrna, now the Gediz. This battle in which the Smyrnaeans beat off the Lydians probably took place in the 660s. We cannot identify the heroic warrior whose qualities Mimnermus contrasts with the feebleness of his hearers.

Alcman

1 *Lykaithos concerns me not*: the obscure figures of Spartan legend mentioned in these lines were probably sons of Hippocoon, usurpers, killed by Castor and Polydeuces. The chorus of girls refers to itself as 'me' in the singular; this is usual in Greek choral song.

Measure and Means: the idea is probably that the advantage goes to those who (unlike the sons of Hippocoon) respect the due measure and do not outreach their means.

a Venetian: it is uncertain whether this refers to the Venetians of the north Adriatic or to a similarly named people in Paphlagonia (north Asia Minor).

the plough: or possibly 'the robe'. Apparently a reference to the accompanying ritual. But the interpretation of the whole sentence is much disputed.

Ainesimbrota's: apparently a woman able to cast love-spells.

Aotis: unknown; perhaps the name of a goddess.

   3 *as to milady Astymeloisa*: in the Greek too there is a play on the girl's name, which means 'on the city's mind'.

   56 *slayer of Argus*: this Homeric title of Hermes seems to have no special relevance here. The point is that he was a herdsmen's god.

Sappho

   15 *Doricha*: a courtesan in the Greek colony of Naucratis in Egypt. Sappho's brother Charaxus, a trader, had become expensively involved with her. Fragments 5 and 15 may come from the same poem.

   17 *Atreus' royal sons*: Agamemnon and Menelaus, according to Lesbian legend, established the local cult of the three deities mentioned in this poem on their way home from Troy.

Thyone's son: Dionysus.

   23 *Hermione*: the daughter of Helen.

   44 *Thebes*: not the city of Oedipus, but a town in the Troad.

Ilus' noble descendants: the Trojans, Ilus being the eponymous hero of Ilios.

   44A *the daughter of Koios*: Leto. Koios was one of the Titans, a brother of Kronos.

   55 *Pieria's roses*: Pieria, north of Mount Olympus, was famed as the birthplace of the Muses.

   99b *son of Zeus and Leto*: Apollo.

   110 *The doorman's feet*: the doorman is guarding the chamber where a newly wed couple have retired. The bride's friends outside, in merry mood, make fun of him.

   134 *the Cyprian goddess*: Aphrodite.

   140 *Adonis is dying*: Adonis, whose name came from the Phoenician *'adôn* ('Lord'), was one form of the Near Eastern god who was the goddess of love's lover and who died and was mourned annually. This is the earliest mention of his cult in Greece. It was popular especially with women. The song is for some kind of ritual play in which Adonis' death was enacted.

   142 *Niobe*: this woman was unwise enough to boast that she had

borne far more children than Leto, who had only two. But those two were Apollo and Artemis, the gods with the power of life and death over boys and girls, and they killed all of Niobe's sons and daughters.

166 *an egg*: no doubt the one from which Helen was reputed to have been born. In the usual version this was the result of Zeus' taking the form of a swan to seduce Leda.

Alcaeus or Sappho

42 *Makar's island*: Lesbos. Makar was its legendary first colonist.

Alcaeus

129 *Aeolian goddess*: Hera. For the trio of deities see the note on Sappho 17.

Hyrrhas' son: Pittacus.

130b *Onomacles*: evidently a figure from recent history, famous as a lone-wolf guerrilla.

70 *the Atreid line*: one noble family in Mytilene, the Penthilidae, claimed descent from Orestes, the son of Agamemnon and grandson of Atreus.

298 *Aias' sacrilege*: this Aias (or Ajax) was the less prominent of the two Homeric heroes bearing this name, the Locrian Aias. His sacrilege is described in the following stanzas.

Priam's daughter: Cassandra.

42 *Aeacus' son*: Peleus. His bride was the sea-nymph Thetis; their son was Achilles. Chiron, a wise and amiable Centaur, was responsible for Achilles' upbringing.

44 *called on his mother's name*: to complain of Agamemnon's overbearing treatment of him in taking away his attractive prisoner of war Briseis. The story is related in book 1 of the *Iliad*, which Alcaeus is concisely summarizing.

395 *Xanthus*: the alternative name of the river Scamander below Troy. Again Alcaeus alludes to a particular episode in the *Iliad* (21. 211–21).

38 *cheating death*: Sisyphus instructed his wife not to perform his funeral rites. A dead person whose funeral has not been properly performed is liable to return as a ghost to haunt the living, and this enabled Sisyphus to escape from the underworld and resume his place on earth. His eventual punishment was to be forever rolling a boulder up a hill, only to see it go tumbling down again.

359 *you void lads of their wits*: boys blew through limpet shells to make

an interesting noise, and the idea is that they blow their own wits
out as they do so. Compare the anonymous elegiac fragment no.
19 (p. 192).

354 *lord of the Scythian land*: in a number of places, especially some of
the Greek colonies in the north of the Black Sea, adjoining Scyth-
ian territory, Achilles was worshipped as a hero. 'Hero' in this
religious context means a dead person whose spirit remains
powerful on earth.

Theognis

12 *founded here*: at Megara. The shrine of Artemis there (like that of
Zeus, Hera, and Dionysus on Lesbos) was reputed to have been
founded by Agamemnon at the time of the Trojan War.

432 *the Asclepiads*: the doctors' union, named after Asclepius the god
of healing.

549 *The silent messenger*: a beacon fire.

Solon

Salamis: this poem originally contained about 100 lines. In it Solon
urged the despondent Athenians not to give up the struggle with
Megara for retention of Salamis; he represented himself as a
herald arrived from the island. We are told that the exhortation
was effective and that Salamis was duly recovered.

2 *Sikinos or Pholegandros*: petty Aegean islands.

4a *the eldest country of Ionia*: Ionia covers Athens and the surrounding
region (Attica), Euboea, most of the islands of the central Aegean,
and most of the Greek colonies on the coast of Anatolia. Athens
claimed to be the earliest inhabited.

10 *how mad I am*: some of Solon's political opponents had impugned
his sanity.

11 *You raised these men up*: the authors who quote these lines sup-
posed the reference to be to the dictatorship of Pisistratus, which
began in about 561. But Solon speaks of plural tyrants—perhaps
some earlier junta of which we know nothing.

13 *Athena's and Hephaestus' craft*: these were patron deities of crafts-
men, at Athens especially of potters.

19 *Cypris*: the goddess of Cyprus, Aphrodite.

20 Solon quotes and criticizes a line of Mimnermus (6. 2), who
appears to be still alive. The name by which he is addressed, Ligy-
astades, may mean 'melodious singer'.

22a *Critias*: son of Solon's brother Dropides, and a great-great-
grandfather of Plato.

36 *from whom I lifted boundary-stones*: Solon had helped those in the poverty trap by a general cancellation of existing debts. The boundary-stones in question had marked mortgaged land.

Attributed to Homer: Margites

5 This appears to be a borrowing from Archilochus (201).

Stesichorus

The Song of Geryon: this poem related one of the major exploits of Heracles, the capture of Geryon's cattle. Geryon or Geryones was a winged monster with three heads, six arms, and six legs, the son of Chrysaor and the nymph Callirhoe. He lived in the far west, on the island of Erythea (probably Cadiz).

184 *Tarshish river*: the Guadalquivir.

185 *the son of Zeus took his way*: to reach Erythea Heracles commandeered the golden bowl in which, according to some poets (cf. Mimnermus 12), the Sun travels at night round Oceanus, the river that encircles the earth, to get back to the east.

181 *Pholos*: a Centaur with whom Heracles stayed as he passed through the mountains of Arcadia. The smell of the wine, never previously opened, attracted other, aggressive Centaurs, whom Heracles had to drive away.

Palinodes: many authors mention a 'Palinode' of Stesichorus in which he retracted what he had previously related about Helen—the usual story that she had eloped to Troy with Paris—and presented a version in which the gods removed her to Egypt for the duration of the Trojan War and duped Paris and everyone else with a phantom Helen. It was said that the goddess Helen had struck Stesichorus blind because of his first account, which did her no credit, and that on composing the Palinode he recovered his sight. One source states that there were two separate Palinodes.

Eriphyle: the poem presumably related how Alcmaeon killed his mother Eriphyle to avenge his father, the seer Amphiaraus, whom she had compelled to take part in a war that he knew would bring his death. Adrastus was Eriphyle's brother.

209 This fragment comes from an account of Telemachus' visit to Sparta to seek news of his father, adapted from book 15 of the *Odyssey*.

217 *this bow*: it was given so that Orestes could defend himself against the Furies when they pursued him because of his murder of his mother.

219 The dream was Clytemnestra's. The serpent represents Agamem-

non, whom she killed (in one version) with an axe. The king that appeared 'out of that' (or perhaps 'after that') is presumably Orestes. Pleisthenes in some traditions replaced Atreus as Agamemnon's father. So the point may be that the legitimate king was to regain the throne from the usurper Aegisthus.

The Hunters of the Boar: heroes from many parts of Greece assembled to help Meleager hunt the mighty boar that the goddess Artemis sent to ravage the land of Calydon. The sons of Thestios were Meleager's uncles.

The Sons of Oedipus: Oedipus having laid curses upon his two sons Polynices and Eteocles, the seer Teiresias has prophesied to Jocasta that they will kill each other. She tries to prevent this by arranging that her sons should separate and rule Thebes in alternation. So Polynices departs. He went to Argos and there married the daughter of the king Adrastus. Later, when Eteocles proved unwilling to cede the Theban throne, Polynices tried with Adrastus' support to return and seize it by force. The two brothers duly killed one another in the battle.

223 *deserters of their men*: Tyndareos' three daughters were Timandra, who left her husband Echemos for another man; Clytemnestra, who was unfaithful to Agamemnon; and Helen, who deserted Menelaus when she sailed away with Paris.

P. Oxy. 3876 fr. 4 *daughter of Thestios*: Althaea. When the Calydonian Boar was killed, Meleager gave its hide to Atalanta, whom he fancied. His uncles, Althaea's brothers, took it away from her, and in a rage he killed them. The subject of the following fragment is obscure.

Ibycus

282 *Polycrates*: see Introduction, p. xvi.

285 *sons of Moliona*: Cteatus and Eurytus, the Siamese twins of Greek

Anacreon

347 *your delightful neck*: the addressee is a Thracian youth called Smerdies. For him and his hair see also fragments 366, 414, and 422.

348 *Lethaeus*: a tributary of the Maeander that flowed past the city of Magnesia. Artemis had a temple nearby.

388 *'Koisyra's son'*: Koisyra was the proverbial *grande dame*.

415 *kottabos*: a popular party game, reputed to come from Sicily, in which drinkers slung the wine-dregs from their cups at a target.

Lasus

702 *Clymenus' consort, the Maid*: Persephone. Clymenus is a name for Hades, the lord of the dead.

Hipponax

3 *Maia's son, Cyllene's sultan*: Hermes, the protecting god of thieves. Cyllene is the mountain in Arcadia where he was born. 'Sultan' translates a Lydian word that Hipponax uses a number of times for comic-bombastic effect.

4a *Amythaonid*: i.e. a claimed descendant of the mythical seer Melampous, the son of Amythaon.

5 *pelted with fig-branches*: this and the five following fragments allude to an Ionian 'scapegoat' ritual in which, to purify the city, some friendless wretch was first given a good meal, then subjected to various indignities, driven out of the town, and (perhaps) put to death.

63 *Myson*: in response to an enquiry as to who was the wisest of men, the Delphic oracle unexpectedly named this obscure person. He was later counted as one of the Seven Sages.

72 *Rhesus*: a Thracian king who arrived at a late stage in the Trojan War to assist the Trojans, but was killed in a night commando raid. The story is told in book 10 of the *Iliad*.

78 *this fellow*: his penis. The narrator presumably gestured towards his own; possibly, like later comic actors, he wore a large artificial phallus.

92 *in Lydian*: the woman is using spells and other measures to treat the narrator for impotence. The transliteration of the Lydian phrase is uncertain, and our knowledge of the language insufficient to elucidate it.

104 *the Thargelia*: the festival that included the 'scapegoat' ritual. Pandora ('All-giver') is here a title of the Earth-goddess.

115 *Salmydessos*: a rocky, harbourless coast on the Black Sea, west of the Bosporus, a region notorious for shipwrecks.

128 *Tell me, O Muse*: this fragment is a parody of the epic style.

129 *Bendova's isle*: the hero of the *Odyssey* spends time on the isle of Calypso; Hipponax substitutes 'Cypso', which has the indelicate meaning indicated by my rendering.

Anonymous Theognidea

692 *to cheer your friends*: I have tried to render a play in the Greek on Chaeron's name, which means 'man of joy'.

702 *the Aeolid Sisyphus*: see the note on Alcaeus 38. Rhadamanthys was a brother of Minos, and famed for his wisdom and justice.

715 *Harpies*: fearsome female wind-demons who carry people off for good. The two sons of Boreas, the North Wind, were also supernatural wind-spirits. According to one myth they pursued the Harpies and eventually caught and killed them.

764 *this Median war*: the poem was composed at a time when a Persian invasion threatened. The date depends on the identity of 'this town'. If it is an Ionian town, it might be as early as 540; if it is in mainland Greece, the reference is most likely to Xerxes' invasion in 480.

774 *on Pelops' son Alcathous' behalf*: this refers to the foundation-myth of Megara. So in this case the Median threat can be fairly safely identified as that of the year 480. The poet may be Philiadas, known as a Megarian poet of that time.

843 *when he that was higher comes to be below*: a mock oracle in solemn style. It probably means 'when the drinker sinks to the floor'.

894 *the clan of Cypselus*: Cypselus and his son Periander were tyrants of Corinth from about 657 to 585. We cannot identify the historical setting of these verses. Cerinthus and the plain of Lelantum were in Euboea; the plain was the scene of repeated conflict in the early historical period.

1024 *Tmolus*: a mountain in Lydia.

1216 *the Lethaean Plain*: see the note on Anacreon 348. But the reference here may be to the symbolic Plain of Lethe (Oblivion), situated in the world of the dead.

1229 *a carcass of the sea*: the poet refers in riddling fashion to a conch, a shell trumpet, being used to send a signal from one house to another.

1232 *Because of you*: Troy was destroyed because of Helen's passion for Paris, but it is not clear which of the stories about Theseus the poet had in mind. For Ajax see Alcaeus, fragment 298.

1288 *Atalanta*: in one version of the myth Atalanta held a spear as she raced against her suitors, and killed all who could not outdistance her. But the following lines show the myth employed with a different point, and they may be the work of a different poet.

Xenophanes

2 *pentathlon*: the ancient pentathlon consisted of discus-throwing, the long jump, the javelin, running, and wrestling.

pankration: a form of unarmed combat in which almost anything was allowed except for biting and eye-gouging.

7a Pythagoras was an (older?) contemporary of Xenophanes. His achievements and teachings are shrouded in legend, but this early anecdote presupposes that he believed in the transmigration of souls between human and animal bodies.

Simonides

507 *That Ram was duly fleeced*: referring to the defeat of a wrestler Krios, whose name meant 'ram'.

509 *son of Alcmena*: Heracles.

511 *the man of Pyrrhus' line*: the noble Thessalian family called the Aleuadai, with whom Simonides was friendly, traced its descent from one Pyrrhus, perhaps identified with Achilles' son Neoptolemus.

515 *daughters of storm-swift mares*: a high-flown periphrasis for 'mules'. The poem celebrated a victory in a mule-cart race at Olympia won by Anaxilas, tyrant of Rhegium.

519 fr. 32 *the goddess*: Leto, mother of Apollo and Artemis.

531 *Leonidas*: the leader of the Spartans who died heroically defending the pass at Thermopylae in 480.

543 *in the carven chest*: when Danae, in spite of all her father's precautions, was impregnated by Zeus and gave birth to Perseus, she and the baby were put out to sea in a chest.

551 *had I come earlier*: the red sail mentioned in 550 was meant to be hoisted as a signal if Theseus returned to Athens successfully from his expedition against the Minotaur, to save Aegeus waiting for the ship to dock. Theseus forgot to hoist it, and his father, assuming the worst, threw himself off the Acropolis. 551 is apparently spoken to Aegeus by a messenger who arrives too late.

555 *the Peleiades*: the star-group known as the Pleiades or Peleiades (the latter form means 'doves') was identified with the seven nymphs who were Atlas' daughters.

595 *their mortal ears*: those of the Argonauts, who, like Odysseus, sailed by the Sirens' island. They were able to overcome the temptation to tarry because they had Orpheus with them, and his singing, described in the following fragment, was sweeter even than that of the Sirens.

577a *Cassotis*: the probable name of a spring at Delphi where the Muses had a shrine. Clio was the senior Muse.

581 *Cleobulus*: later considered one of the Seven Sages; here treated as the author of a famous epitaph for King Midas of Phrygia—

otherwise ascribed to Homer—which declared that the bronze
statue over the tomb would remain

> so long as fountains spring and tall trees grow,
> so long as sun and bright moon rise and shine,
> and rivers run, and sea-waves wash the shore.

587 *fi-ire*: Simonides spread the word for fire, *pyr*, over two or three
musical notes, probably to imitate its flickering.

602 *the empty-headed claim of boys*: these lines are said to have been
composed in criticism of a competition judge who had awarded
a prize to the younger poet Pindar instead of to Simonides.

ELEGIES

3 *Zetes and Kalaïs*: the two supernatural sons of the North Wind,
Boreas. The Athenians are said to have prayed to Boreas before
the battle of Artemisium, and in response he roused the three-day
storm which wrecked a good portion of the Persian navy.

10 *O son of sea-nymph*: Achilles, son of Thetis. This elegy began with
a lengthy proemium addressed to the hero.

11 *and by Menelaus' strength*: the legendary king Menelaus, Agamem-
non's brother, was worshipped at Sparta as a hero. Like the Tynd-
arids, Castor and Polydeuces, he was imagined still to have
power to help his people, and images of all three were carried
with the army.

the Iamid: Tisamenus, the army's official priest and diviner, claimed des-
cent from the ancient seer Iamus.

13 *Dorus*: the ancestor of the Dorians. On the connection with Her-
acles' family see the notes on Tyrtaeus 2 and 19.

14 *the river*: the Asopus. This prophecy by Tisamenus before the
battle of Plataea is recorded by Herodotus (9. 36).

19 *the Chian said*: the Chian is Homer, Chios being one of the chief
claimants to the honour of having been his birthplace. The verse
quoted is from the *Iliad*, 6. 146.

25 *The stuff*: snow, used for cooling wine. 'Buried alive' refers to its
storage underground. Simonides is said to have improvised this
elegant riddle on a hot summer evening when he saw others get-
ting their wine chilled.

26 *broad as it was*: a similar story tells that Simonides came out with
this verse (adapted from *Iliad* 14. 33) when he saw other guests
being served with hare and himself being missed out.

92 Simonides rearranges the same words to make two verses in dif-
ferent metres. See Timocreon, elegiac/iambic fragment 10, for a
rude comment in the same format.

Pratinas

708 *What commotion is this?*: Pratinas' chorus is indignant about a novel form of dithyramb—perhaps due to Lasus—characterized by greater elaboration of the *aulos* accompaniment.

712 *Ionian Muse*: a technical reference to musical modes called 'tense Ionian' and 'slack Ionian'.

Anonymous Party Songs

893 *Harmodius and Aristogeiton*: see Introduction, p. xix.

907 *Leipsydrion*: a place some miles to the north of Athens. In 513 BC a band of dissidents hostile to Hippias' regime, led by the Alcmeonid family, built themselves a fort there. It was besieged and taken by forces from the city. The song was presumably composed soon afterwards, and before the fall of Hippias in 510.

Telesilla

717 *fleeing from Alpheus*: the Alpheus was the principal river of the Peloponnese, flowing westward through Arcadia and Elis. According to a local myth, the river-god pursued the virgin goddess Artemis, but she evaded him.

Timocreon

727 This piece was probably composed in about 478. The men named are Spartans and Athenians who played leading roles in the battles of Salamis (480), Plataea, and Mycale (479). After Salamis, Themistocles had sailed about the Aegean with a fleet on his own initiative, demanding money with menaces from those islands that had collaborated with the Persians, and generally throwing his weight about.

at the Isthmus: the Greek commanders met there to decide which of them had earned the highest honours in the war. Themistocles apparently tried to win favour by laying on a banquet, but the gathering ended inconclusively.

729 About ten years later Themistocles was denounced for involvement in secret dealings with Persia, and Timocreon composed this gleeful song, of which 728 was the opening.

10 *Cean blather*: referring to Simonides' *jeu d'esprit*, elegiac fragment 92; see the note on it above.

Euenus

2 *a foursome with three water-nymphs*: in other words, one part of wine should be mixed with three of water.

8b *the Melian sea*: the island of Melos, from a Parian's viewpoint, marked the beginning of a dangerously exposed stretch of open sea.

Iambic Fragments

1 *Syloson*: younger brother of Polycrates, after whose death in 522 he was installed by Darius as puppet ruler of Samos. His misrule caused many to depart, leaving 'plenty of space'.

Elegiac Fragments

6 *Kedon*: an Athenian remembered for having made some sort of attempt to overthrow Hippias.

17 *Aristomenes*: remembered in Messenian tradition as the great hero of their second war against Sparta in the time of Tyrtaeus.

Melic Fragments

942 *Polyhymnia*: one of the Muses.

1004 *the Tyndarid brothers*: Castor and Polydeuces were particularly associated with saving sailors in peril on the sea. See Alcaeus' hymn to them, fragment 34.

Play Songs

861 We do not know the nature of this game, only that it was played at Tarentum.

875 This was the Pot game. One child sat in the middle and was the Pot. Another ran round the Pot anticlockwise, keeping one hand on the Pot's head. The others hit at him as he went round, while he tried to kick them. If he succeeded, the one kicked took his place. The first part of each verse was sung by the teasers, the second part by the orbiter.

876a *Blind Man's Buff*: one child, blindfolded, ran about reciting the first verse and trying to catch the rest, who belaboured him with papyrus lashes and answered with the second verse. Whoever he caught took his place.

876b *Shine, sun, we love you*: children clapped their hands and chanted this verse if a cloud passed over the sun.

876c *Torty-tortoise*: a girls' game. One, the Tortoise, sat in the middle, while the others ran round her in a circle and questioned her. At the word 'JUMPED' she leapt up to catch whoever was nearest at that moment.

Ritual Songs

848 *the swallow is here*: a children's begging-chant from Rhodes. On a day in spring the children would carry a (model?) swallow with them and go collecting from door to door with this 'trick or treat' manifesto. Similar things are known to have existed elsewhere in Greece, and parallels are found in other parts of Europe.

851a *make way for the god*: a huge wooden phallus, borne into the theatre, perhaps on Delos, by men wearing costumes that included 'masks of drunken men'.

854 *Rain, dear Zeus, rain*: an Athenian prayer.

856 *Come along now, all you sons*: chanted at Spartan military parades, or perhaps when actually on the way to battle.

862 *A holy boy is born*: a proclamation made during the nocturnal rites at the Eleusinian Mysteries. Brimo and Brimos are esoteric cult names for Demeter and Plutus (= Wealth, embodied in the new corn). *Brim-* suggests 'mighty'.

868 *To Athens let us go*: sung by dancing girls of the Bottiaioi, a Macedonian people, at a certain sacrifice.

870 *Young, valiant warriors we used to be*: these lines were recited respectively by groups of old men, able-bodied men, and boys on parade at a Spartan festival.

871 *Come to the festival, O Dionysus*: sung by women of Elis. Dionysus is identified with the bull to be sacrificed—a bull 'worthy' of the god and the occasion.

872 *Put off our old age till later*: at Sparta there was a cult of 'Aphrodite who postpones old age'. The verse may come from there.

877 *O Maiden*: Persephone. The bridge was one crossed by those going from Athens to Eleusis for the celebration of the Mysteries. The triple ploughing of fallow land in the course of the spring and summer made it fully ready for sowing in the autumn.

879 (1) A call and response at the Athenian Lenaea festival. (2) A call and response at Athenian libations. (3) A call following a libation.

881b *Out you go, croaky crow*: chanted at weddings; translation and interpretation doubtful.

882 *Take good fortune*: the conclusion of another collecting-song, sung in the villages round Syracuse by men wearing horns and garlands. They carried bags of mixed seeds and skins full of wine, from which they made token offerings on behalf of those they encountered. 'The goddess' is Artemis.

INDEX OF POETS